It *doesn't* have to be this way

A critique of, and alternatives for,
Australia's current neoliberal,
ecocidal, and greed-capitalist economics

BOB ELLISTON

CONTENTS

About the author *iv*
To get your attention *1*
Climate change, *aka* global heating *4*
Back to economics *7*
Inflation *9*
A better narrative *11*
The analogy *14*
The advantage of privilege *15*
Some history of economics is needed *17*
Keynesianism *22*
Monetarism *26*
Privatisation *29*
Modern Monetary Theory *32*
Fiscal inequity between the tiers of government *39*
Debt *41*
Interest rates *45*
Fascism *49*
    Inflation again *53*
Cost of living *55*
The Market is another pocket deity *58*
The job description of a currency *60*
    Price-gouging – again *64*
The Deficit Myth, budget deficit or surplus and austerity *65*
Mortgage stress *66*
Unaffordable housing *66*
Rent-rise crisis *67*
Homelessness in Australia *69*
Mediocre ALP *70*
Wages and welfare *78*
Unemployment and underemployment *79*
Energy prices *80*
Gross inequality *81*
Poverty *84*

National Debt *86*
Taxation *88*
War-making and a war economy *93*
War begets war *97*
Whose values? *101*
Socialism for the military *104*
Steady-state economy *106*
It's the *ecology*, stupid! *108*
Geoengineering *109*
Nuclear? Yeah nah! *113*
Climate change again *117*
Global heating solutions? *117*
Regarding that cultural motivation *118*
Water security *131*
Food security *131*
Fuel security *132*
Disaster resistant regenerative agriculture and aquaponics *133*
Energy *133*
Immigration and population *134*
Self-sufficiency and recycling *135*
False fears of recession and contraction *135*
Australia's economic base, and tariffs *137*
Another way to think of economics *138*
Economic growth = existential threat *138*
Agriculture *139*
Employment *143*
Population *144*
Conclusions *146*
Preparing *149*

Post script *151*

ABOUT THE AUTHOR

Bob Elliston is a retired nurse whose interest in economics arose thirty years ago when politicians voted themselves a 40% pay rise while Tasmania's Health Department made drastic 'Economic Rationalist' staff cuts at his hospital. These events coincided with Tasmania's conservation struggles and the growing awareness that human-induced climate change poses an even greater danger to our existence than the threat of 'nuclear overkill' that has overhung the world all Bob's life. Exploration of philosophy, economics, religion and ecology, plus a diverse working life, has convinced him that although we face terrifying problems there are still choices and the worst outcomes may yet be averted.

TO GET YOUR ATTENTION

On 23rd October 2023, the EU Tax Observatory EUTAX reported that rich Australians hold over $370 billion in overseas tax havens. The same day, the Foodbank Hunger Report estimated 3.7 million Australian households were unable to afford nutritious food. 23% of Australians are living in severe food insecurity, and 48% are anxious about affording their grocery bill. It's coincidental both numbers include 3 and 7, but food poverty is no coincidence. Inequality, poverty, and unemployment are politico-economic *choices* by our governments and by we voters who elect them. It doesn't have to be this way.

This booklet is mostly about economics because so much that we're doing to the world is based on our economics. It was largely written for Australia in 2023–24, but it applies more widely. The aim is to share what I've learnt so far.

If you're deeply worried for your children's future in the face of rampant militarism, bloody wars and global heating, that's fully justified. If you suspect our capitalist system is faulty, that shows you believe in evidence. If you doubt the link between higher interest rates and the stated aim of stopping supermarkets from raising prices, you're right to be skeptical. If you suspect record bank and corporate profits have a lot to do with the high cost of living, you're not a conspiracist. If you're uneasy about the growing number of billionaires ruling the world, and wondering why they're allowed to pollute the atmosphere more with their super yachts, private jets, and even space rockets, while you worry about your own pollution footprint, then you are not alone. And if you're angry at the way capitalism is ruining the world, then you're right to feel that way, but please do *not* do what xenophobes and Trumpists do, and that's blame immigrants, refugees, or minorities. It's not their fault.

The truth is that our economic system is geared to make the rich richer. It's built to make unfair inequality worse. It's made to enable the theft of the labour and resource wealth of your country by foreign-owned corporations, which carelessly pollute, destroy, and export most or all of their profits. Our economic and industrial system is not designed to care for everybody fairly. Instead, it is trashing our Spaceship Earth, and may soon cause the death of everything on it. The much-lauded economic growth is only increasing our production, consumption, and pollution, but our pollution is poisoning the biosphere which feeds us. And it's an under-reported fact that toxic chemicals are destroying Earth's life-support systems. Cosmetics are killing coral; plankton are lost to plastics; insecticides are causing catastrophic decline in that foundation of our food chain; our herbicides are poisoning us too, and we have very few years left to reverse all that. Everything must change!

Global heating means we have to change almost everything about the way we live. That includes how we grow our food, employ ourselves, and how we distribute wealth. Earth sciences are showing irrefutable evidence that we must switch from a market-based, industrial economic system to needs-based economies with people and Nature at the centre. Sadly, at present most of the wealth produced by our ecocidal economic growth is going to the wealthy. Civilization is metaphorically in a state of terminal obesity. The 'fat' is poorly distributed and clogging up the 'heart' of our society. The only cure for this is a fair and even 'weight reduction' that some are calling 'degrowth'. But to achieve that benign contraction, we need to understand both economics and ecology well enough.

We need people-supportive and Nature-friendly, fair economic systems. We also need people-supportive and science-friendly cultural philosophies to support our restorative efforts. We need to be sufficiently science-literate so that a mass movement of us will be inspired to drive Earth-saving change. And, as odd as it may seem to rational people, that improved cultural philosophy requires devising better religion, where religion is defined broadly as the beliefs and practices that help us to find meaning in daily living. The task, then, is to determine, in light of our many problems, how we can all live well.

I admit I'm *not* an economist. As a retired nurse, by default I'm one of Australia's millions of share-bludgers. My interest in economics grew from a commitment to fairness and a hope to see economic and social justice. It was also spurred by seeing xenophobes blame minority groups for the economic damage done by neoliberal economic globalisation. It's obvious that we need an economics for need, not greed. The present cost-of-living crunch is largely due to greed. Profiteering is behind recent price hikes because profiteering has become a global sport. While many would disagree, I argue that excessive profit amounts to theft. I believe profiteering is anti-social, anti-human and inexcusable.

Our current problems are caused by our economic system, and we cannot continue with this flawed system while the growing damage from global heating hits us. As global heating takes its toll and strangles the supply of food and essentials, there will be challenging price rises (*aka* inflation) and the cost of living will become a worsening struggle. The cost of living is bad enough now, but if the present profiteering is allowed to continue into these future struggles, then it will only compound that cost.

But it doesn't have to be that way. Up to the time of writing the Reserve Bank of Australia (RBA) has raised our interest rates thirteen times and is resisting calls to lower them again. But they didn't need to raise the interest rates at all because, as we'll see later, higher interest rates tend to *increase* inflation more than lower it, and the higher rates cause a lot of needless damage in society. There is a way to limit price rises to those that are strictly necessary, but it requires governments to exercise their powers for the benefit of citizens and their economy. An example where a government took control of prices was in 1941 when US President F. D. Roosevelt feared profiteering and high inflation would result from the economic effort to fight World War II. His Executive Order 8875 established the Office of Price Administration (OPA), which reasonably controlled profiteering by capping prices and rationing consumption. Governments should copy that example now.

My argument is that we must adjust everything about how we operate, firstly so that we will be ***able*** to fight the biggest fight humanity will ever face (ecological breakdown from global heating), and secondly so that, as the disasters increase, it's not just all the poorest people dying first and the rich being the last humans to exist. So, one aim of this booklet is to give the reader enough information to make you feel angry, as I am, then to inspire you to demand radical Earth-saving action – and also to join the multi-faceted reformation and restoration of civil society that we must create – or else accept our extinction.

As the subtitle says, this is a critique of economics and an offering of alternatives for Australia's current system, plus global capitalism in general. It grew from a hastily written submission to the Australian Government's 2022 review of the Reserve Bank of Australia (RBA). That became submission number 51.

That submission needed to be broader and more accessible. It included trenchant criticism of our RBA and of the neoliberal, monetarist, economic dogma Australia and other countries are suffering from. My critique of the harmful RBA is just a small part of a deeper desire for truth, fairness, and survival. This booklet is a miniaturised and localised version of my yet-to-be-published book called *Liberation Economics*. It examines our existential threats, namely: global heating, nuclear weapons and other modes of mass murder, plus militarism. And I explain why (contrary to our current economics) 'economic growth' is one of a handful of existential threats. A fifth major threat is also examined in detail.

CLIMATE CHANGE, *aka* GLOBAL HEATING

Global heating is the ecocidal result of our economics. Before I explain some economics, though, it's vital to explain global heating. There's been a tragic failure of education about climate change and the danger it poses to this biosphere that we all depend on. Far from the problem being exaggerated, there's been a deliberate campaign to obstruct understanding and to minimize climate action. Governments have not faced down this cynical deception. We've been fed inadequate information and blatant lies, which together have fostered doubt, disbelief, and denial. Having read enough genuine climate science, I have to say there's very bad news. Earth used to be in a beautiful energy balance where the energy it gained from the sun was equal to the energy it lost to space. This balance was maintained by the living biosphere itself: what we call Nature. Our pollution of Earth's relatively thin atmosphere, with all the carboniferous fuels we've dug up and burnt to power our industrialisation, plus our vast deforestation, plus the pollution and acidification of the seas, has caused that balance to be lost. Our growing industrial economies have, ironically, caused the very pollution that is set to end our industrial civilisation.

By pollution, I mean the plastics and toxic chemicals that are trashing the oceans and, of course, the products of combustion of fossil fuels that have unbalanced the greenhouse effect. Many people still don't understand 'the greenhouse effect', but we owe our lives and our whole evolution to this warming blanket effect of Earth's atmosphere. If kept in balance that's a good thing, but since that balance has been lost all life on Earth is in danger.

To try to make this phenomenon easier to grasp, I'll offer the example of the 'hot car effect' as a more widely familiar demonstrator. Radiation of many frequencies comes from the Sun, but especially the higher-frequency, ultra-violet, more penetrating light (called insolation) stimulates objects on Earth's surface to emit low-frequency infra-red (heat) radiation that can't get back out to the absolute cold of space because the 'greenhouse' gasses are opaque to that low frequency (heat) radiation. Earth's atmosphere is like the car windows: it traps heat. Our gaseous pollution has tinted 'the window', wrecking Earth's delicate energy balance almost irrevocably. The heating has been compounded by itself, so the planet is now self-heating via feedback loops. Not only is more heat being trapped than is able to escape to space, but, due to the shrinkage of melting glaciers and the loss of sea ice, their whiteness (albedo) effect is reflecting less UV light back to space. Add to this the fact that the melting of arctic permafrost has released a lot of methane, which is worse than CO_2 at trapping heat in the short term. Global heating may become CH_4-led more than CO_2-led.

Most of the heat and much of our carboniferous pollution has been absorbed by the oceans, to date, but that is making it all worse – it's causing the oceans to become both hotter and more acidic, and these rapidly changing conditions are making life difficult for all sorts of marine life, especially the photosynthesising plankton that recycle much of Earth's oxygen. And we must stop killing whales and dolphins because they help the plankton.

Here are two simple explanations of global heating that even Andrew Bolt might understand:

>https://www.youtube.com/watch?v=NTbR8omNbVY
>https://www.youtube.com/watch?v=bu3J0oDuNwQ

The result of this heating effect is increasing weather-related disasters, globally and locally. Yet still the commercial media and the old political parties in Australia are acting as if a US war on China over Taiwan is the biggest threat to Australia. Consider recent events in Australia: the Summer of Fires (2019–2020), East Coast floods (Lismore), Murray Basin flood, Kimberley floods, Gulf-country floods, and North Queensland floods at Christmas 2023. Now recall the Summer heat-waves in the Northern hemisphere, mega-fires in Canada, Greece, and Hawaii, the powerful typhoons and hurricanes, and the year's-worth of rain that fell in 8 hours on Valencia in October 2024. These increasing, 'unprecedented' events are all made record-breaking by the heating. Scientists who collect the data on average temperatures tell us that 2023 was the hottest year on record so far. Maybe 2023 was the year Earth broke through the 1.5° C above the 10,000 year-old pre-industrial average. Australia busted the 1.5° C level in 2023 and scientists are unhappily confident that the globe will exceed the 1.5° C level in 2024. However research published on 6th February 2024 suggests we exceeded 1.5° of heating ten years ago. Scientists analyzed 300 years of ocean temperature records from sea sponges and showed we may be above 1.7° C now and still rising irreversibly:

>https://www.nature.com/articles/s41558-023-01919-7

What all real climate scientists will agree on is the frightening speed of the global temperature rise. Where the degree of change we are seeing took thousands of years in the past, we have compressed it into decades because our pollution has unbalanced the system. The IPCC Report published on 20th March 2023 made it clear there's a gaping chasm between present climate policies and the climate action and pro-Nature action that's needed. It's the same in many countries, but despite having a better government since 2022, it's still sadly true in Australia. We're not doing nearly enough! The report states that "without a strengthening of policies, global warming of 3.2° C is projected by 2100." It may get worse than that. If you are not yet convinced, I give you these videos to watch:

The late professor Will Steffen talks to Laura Tingle on *7.30* 29th January 2021.

> https://www.youtube.com/watch?v=_E1koGztlkE

Video on climate change speaking of 1.3 degrees already and what 3 degrees might be like:

> https://www.youtube.com/watch?v=uynhvHZUOOo

The long story on anthropogenic Global Heating, 1st September 2023:

> https://www.youtube.com/watch?v=dpvd9FensT8

Global heating is not going to stop when we get to zero emissions. The atmospheric load of greenhouse gasses will maintain the heating of the biosphere. As mentioned above, several climate dominoes have fallen such as ocean acidification and the Arctic permafrost. Tragically, these won't reverse even when or if Nature starts reducing the greenhouse gasses. Only if or when the biosphere gets below pre-industrial settings and the oceans are able to lose some of the heat they've gained, only then might global temperatures re-stabilise. However, without every key pillar of the global biosphere, the whole system is destined for collapse. The big problem at the intersection of global heating and climate **in**action is that the longer the heating processes go unchecked the harder it's going to be for our children to reverse the problem. Every day of business-as-usual makes the problem of climate change worse. We science-literate folks get called alarmists, but if you're not alarmed you are either ignorant, stupid, or both! Every government everywhere should be treating global heating with the utmost urgency. If knowing these things doesn't make all nations redirect every effort into reducing our pollution, then we truly don't care about our children, or even ourselves! While progress is happening that total re-direction of effort is yet to occur. Most governments are doing not enough or are simply practicing complacent inaction.

Many people have been given the impression that it is only sea-level rise that is the problem, and certainly most members of Australia's federal Liberal/Labor duopoly seem to act as if there's nothing worse that could happen. People can step back from rising seas, and what are a few million climate refugees from Pacific islands? Sea-level rise is a problem, but it may be the least of our worries. What the increasingly severe weather disasters will do to our agriculture and to our food and water supply systems is the biggest danger.

The reasons why governments are not doing enough on climate change are many and varied. The many reasons for climate science denial is a subject others have thought and written about, and this booklet won't try to add to that. Just to say that most people simply don't want to know about climate change. It's too hard to contemplate. We may lack enough imagination to extrapolate what's happening now and see what will happen in the near future. Also, the campaign of denial and the sowing of doubt has been very successful, so politicians are still being driven by fossil fuel corporations and right-wing sceptics rather than by a mass movement of voters. The pro-money, anti-life resistance is powerful and wealthy. And even among the convinced, it's a minority of people who are up for such an overwhelming fight as saving the planet. Plus, the word 'crisis' has been pinned on both climate change and the high cost of living, as if these things will reach a peak and then the crisis will pass, but both these challenges are only going to get worse and compound each other as climate destruction drives up prices. Neither will be ameliorated unless we all push for radical change.

In her 2014 book, *This Changes Everything*, Naomi Klein put it this way:

> *Our economic system and our planetary system are now at war. Or, more accurately, our economy is at war with many forms of life on earth, including human life. What the climate* [the biosphere] *needs to avoid collapse is a contraction in humanity's use of resources. What our* [current] *economic model demands to avoid collapse is unfettered expansion. Only one of these sets of rules can be changed, and it's not the laws of Nature.*

It's so obvious that it's our economics that has to change, yet there is still huge political resistance to this fact.

The single worst crime of all governments is to fail to treat global heating seriously enough. We absolutely must stop using and wasting fossil fuels, and that includes stopping that huge and totally needless emitter, the global military industrial complex. War-making is the single most wasteful, anti-economic, polluting and anti-human thing we do. It doesn't have to be that way! World Peace would be a big help right now.

However, as Naomi Klein and others have emphasised, this threat to life on Earth could just possibly be our best-ever chance to build a better world – one in which politico-economic ideology, disinformation, and cruel militarism are transcended, and in which reason, truth, peace and kindness are manifest in a new reformation of our global civilisation.

BACK TO ECONOMICS

As I said, almost everything we are doing to the biosphere is grounded in our economics, but we'll have to delve into cultural aspects too. On one level culture is 'just how we do things'. Another definition is that it's our 'beliefs, practices and traditions'. Culture is our 'way of being' which deserves deep consideration. But culture is also about our attitudes and behaviours. To change enough to save ourselves, we have to modify our attitudes and behaviours, and especially be more tolerant of others. Later I'll discuss our 'culturally acquired maladaptive behaviours', of which our economic system is one.

Hot topics in 2023 included the ***interest rate rises*** imposed by the RBA. On November 7th that year they raised interest rates for the thirteenth time, supposedly to slow the relentless inflation/price-rises that are causing ***rising-cost-of-living anxiety*** to all normal wage earners. I'll seek to show that the present cost of living struggle wasn't and isn't being caused by external issues like Covid supply-chain blockages or Northern wars, so much as by bad actors here in Australia. The price-setters have been caught out price-gouging by the fact that many corporations have made record profits since the '***rising-rates & inflation spiral***' began causing financial pain, in 2022. The ***price rises*** and CPI increase got to an average 7% annually while wage rises (for those privileged enough to gain them) nudged 3% per annum. Most workers were (and still are) going backwards financially. The Coles-Woolworths supermarket duopoly was shown to have been ripping off their customers and bully-squeezing their suppliers in the pursuit of maximum profit. Plus, the rising interest rates have caused '***mortgage stress***' to the approximately 500,000 home buyers who now don't know how they'll be able to pay so much more money to the banks without joining the growing numbers of ***homeless people*** in Australia. And while much homelessness is caused by the chronic ***lack of affordable housing***, it is compounded by ***rent-gouging landlords*** and our epidemic of ***domestic violence***. In this resource-rich country it's estimated there are 3.32 million people (13.4% of the population), including 761,000 or 16.6% of children, are living in poverty – 1 in 8 of our population of 27 million. Abject poverty is a loss of liberty second only to imprisonment, yet our federal government refuses to raise welfare payments (notably Jobseeker), not even up to the poverty line as defined by the OECD.

Here is the 2023 report on poverty and inequality from ACOSS:

> https://povertyandinequality.acoss.org.au/poverty-in-australia-2023-who-is-affected/

Here is the ACOSS report on poverty from 2024:

> https://www.acoss.org.au/wp-content/uploads/2024/10/241014-ACOSS-policy-solutions-to-poverty-for-Anti-Poverty-Week.pdf

And here's what The Brotherhood of St Laurence has found:

> https://www.bsl.org.au/bsl-drives-change/poverty-in-australia/

Many people recognise the ***extreme inequality*** that now exists, and many people realise that ***gender inequality*** is compounding ***domestic violence*** and the epidemic of ***femicide***. About a third of ***suicides*** in Australia are on an income support benefit. But not enough people are yet identifying the deep cultural and economic causes of these problems or taking effective action to fix them. It seems the majority of politicians in our Liberal/Labor political duopoly are careless of the intersecting causes of all our social problems. And likewise the board of the (supposedly) independent RBA – people who cannot know the sheer despair they cause in the financial stress they inflict on others. Yet they have the hide to claim that *more* people should be unemployed in order to hobble wage justice and to reduce inflation. This is because workers can't buy so much when they're unemployed, so that's supposed to reduce business profits enough to restrain price rises – nonsense!

INFLATION

Inflation is essentially price-rises. The inflation *rate* is the speed at which prices are rising. If prices stop rising (even though staying high), then inflation falls to zero. Rising prices (inflation) cause the purchasing power of your wage-dollar to fall. The opposite is called deflation, and the deflation rate is the measure of the speed of price falls. Deflation gives your wages a little more purchasing power, so businesses will do everything to avoid that. And our RBA likes to keep prices rising and the value of your wages falling for the same reason. They chose the 2–3% band as the inflation rate and annual loss of purchasing power that we could learn to tolerate. Recent higher inflation caused workers to have more than usual financial pain, and this has caused embarrassment for governments.

Climate disasters are adding to all these problems, but at base each problem is a failure of 'The Market', and of neoliberal economics, to serve the best interests of every citizen. People are sick of the paltry and/or foolish action on all these problems and are demanding that governments take responsibility and do whatever it takes to fix things. And they know that the only proper cure for such failures is for the people's government to have the courage and wit to truly serve the interests of *all* its citizens, not just the wealthy few.

Sadly, both major political parties are wedded to neoliberal economics, at both federal and state levels. This duet of adherence to 'orthodox' economics and political dogma is preventing the fixing of many problems. The two-party duopoly is failing us. At a state level it's neoliberalism that's behind ambulance ramping, the lack of affordable homes, the shortage of affordable GP services, and poor outcomes in public schools. At a federal level, right-wing forces are trying to "make life difficult for the ALP government", as Dutton once put it. The evidence for that is in the lying attacks by the America-owned Murdoch media and in the disinformation from outfits organised by the billionaire-backed Atlas Network, such as the IPA, ASPI, 'Advance' and many others. It's plausible that right-wing groups are conspiring to defend neoliberalism and the American influence in Australia. The evidence is in the savage and needless interest-rate rises, the price-gouging supermarkets, needless hikes in energy prices and in the housing shortage that makes governments look weak and incompetent – which is exactly the intention of neoliberal ideology.

Making governments small and weak is a stated aim of neoliberalism. The past L/NP regime was guilty of wrecking-crew politics. In July 2022, David Ritter, CEO of Greenpeace Australia, referred on Twitter to Thomas Frank's 2008 book *The Wrecking Crew*. The author coined the idea of 'wrecking crew' politicians – those who:

> *... deliberately or recklessly seek to govern badly in order to advance an extreme ideological agenda. The aim of 'wrecking crew' politics is that the whole idea of government is damaged and discredited. People stop believing in the power of government to do helpful things – and may even stop believing*
> *in the whole idea of the public good.*

It is my sincere opinion that many wreckers in the federal L/NP coalition are not people of good intention.

Evidence that dark forces are doing their best to make the federal ALP look bad is in the fact that the ALP is struggling to adequately address the issues of global heating, poverty, and inequality. The federal ALP is sending mixed messages in many areas: they talk about saving Nature, but still allow growth in the fossil-fuel industries; they talk about Australia being a mature country, yet allow News Corp to continue its disinformation/propaganda. They've handed our sovereignty to the American military via the on-going Force Posture Agreement between Australia and the United States, and the ALP is persisting with AUKUS.

This critique of our economics will also include a criticism of the political parties and the failings of politics in Australia. Our democracy needs more independent politicians who lead innovation while truly hearing their communities. And we need a dramatic return to truth in our society rather than continuing to allow falsehoods and lying scare campaigns to dominate our politics. All our communication media – traditional and social media – must be fact-checked rigorously. Allowing divisive, Trump-style, baseless opinions to have free rein will only make us unable to solve our many problems. Truthfulness may be difficult to achieve, but we must try.

Certainly federal Labor has done many good things since Australians voted for change in 2022, but there's much more to be done. Are they to blame? Perhaps corporate-lobbyists and left-over L/NP advisors have ill-advised the ALP. Our public service has largely been privatised to dodgy 'consulting firms', like PWC, and corrupted by cronyism. The ALP government has approved far too many fossil fuel projects when none were warranted. Fear of attacks from the right-wing media has made the ALP timid. Sadly, there's been a 'small-target' policy ever since Labor was rejected in 2019. But even after achieving government federal Labor has shown little courage on issues like restoring Medicare, funding public housing, or funding public schools equally to private schools. They nearly failed to save Julian Assange from the US (a last minute plea-bargain saved him). They've failed at ensuring justice for public service whistle-blowers and failed to create an open NACC that will prosecute all the corrupt members of the elite (e.g. those guilty of Robodebt and the Army generals overseeing wars crimes). The ALP is also irrationally pro-US and sycophantic in continuing AUKUS – a mere ego-trip and vanity-fest of the L/NP. Has our government been infiltrated by toxic powers? We've *again* been sucked into the warmonger-hegemony of the USA, our 'dangerous ally', as former PM, Malcolm Fraser correctly labeled America. Australia's proper name is the Commonwealth of Australia – there's an egalitarian idea behind that. It comes from 'common' and 'weal' or wealth, and signifies common well-being, fairness, or common good. But Labor is now a right-wing party. Many Australians would prefer an egalitarian democracy, equal rights for all, common prosperity, and future-focused, independent MPs.

A BETTER NARRATIVE

We need a better notion of ourselves than the self-serving, selfish, 'homo-economicus' narrative, and the only way to defeat a faulty narrative is to create a much better one. Ironically, we humans are at once the most sublime and savage animal on Earth. We're also members of a species of large ape that is still trying to civilize itself. Many will recoil at that statement, but apes we are, and our uncivilized side is proven by our war-making. We may have come far, but we will either become wise or go extinct. This sounds gloomy, but it's the truest narrative that we can honestly adopt. Yet we can be our sublime selves and maximise the sociable, creative, co-operative and caring side of ourselves instead of manifesting the greedy, murdering war-criminal side of ourselves.

It's up to us to deserve to inhabit this almost perfect planet by finally learning to live on it kindly, gently, and without killing everything – or each other, as we do. Here are two truths to consider: this is our heavenly haven-home and there is no other. This Earth is our heaven, but some people, and perhaps too many people, are making it hellish.

War is hell yet we keep making war. Why? The accelerating global heating we've caused will turn Spaceship Earth into another kind of hell if we don't turn 180 degrees from what we're doing. But if we all act co-operatively to strive for peace, rationality, and truth, and work to restore Nature, we can still rescue our once-heavenly home. We can turn this unfair and unsustainable dystopia into a fair and sustainable good-place – our eutopia.

Be assured, this is not suggesting perfection in a no-place utopia, but simply aiming for a world that's a good-place (eu-topia), where the biosphere has been restored, our pollution has been stopped and cleaned up, where global peace has been secured, and where our societies are organised for the needs of everyone, not merely for the greeds of the few.

The reader may be unfamiliar with these two 20th century books, but my idea of a eutopia would be more like Khalil Gibran's loving, altruistic society in *The Prophet* rather than the selfish dystopia in Ayn Rand's *Atlas Shrugged*. We need to live by the most loving morality rather than for getting the most money. And we must commit to never-ending mass action sufficient to turn around global ecological breakdown, which is worsening by the day. Millions of species, including our crops and fisheries, cannot adapt to the rapidly changing climate and ecological conditions we've caused. So change is unavoidable. All we can do is take control of this Titanic and try to steer away from the worst destruction.

Science writer Julian Cribb, author of the highly recommended *How to Fix a Broken Planet* (2023), identifies ten interlinked threats:

1. extinction and ecocide – the destruction of the Earth's life support systems
2. resource depletion – depletion of fresh water, soil, forests, fish and other key resources
3. global poisoning – universal chemical pollution
4. global overheating – accelerating climate change
5. a new nuclear arms race – featuring dangerous new weapons, AI and killer robots
6. food insecurity – weakening of farming and marine food systems and supply chains
7. overpopulation – human numbers vastly outrunning the Earth's carrying capacity
8. new pandemic diseases – arising out of ruined environments and science lab
9. uncontrolled technologies – like AI, biotech, nanotech and universal surveillance
10. misinformation and mass delusion – paralysing our ability to act to save ourselves.

Here are two edited versions of what Julian Cribb has said about the last of these. In his blog Surviving C21 and in his essay entitled 'World War Three Begins', he posits that spreading lies is a new World War, even against those who spread the lies themselves:

Potentially, the most deadly of these is mass delusion. The spread of lies and disinformation renders it almost impossible for us to take concerted action to arrest the other nine catastrophic risks. Lies paralyze governments, destabilise politics, lead to war, rot democracy, spread mistrust, destroy public faith in science, and nullify rational decision-making. This torrent of fabrication and falsehood is driven by: the $7 trillion petro-lobby, by corrupt media, venal politicians, ideological extremists, rabid conspiracists. ... and increasing numbers of citizens cannot tell truth from fiction.

In his essay *The Age of Deceit*, Julian Cribb quotes the authors of the Doomsday clock:

This wanton disregard for science and the large-scale embrace of conspiratorial nonsense – often driven by political figures and partisan media – undermined the ability of responsible national and global leaders to protect the security of their citizens,
adding,
The dissemination of lies increased the danger from established threats like nuclear weapons, climate change, and pandemic disease.

Disinformation must be confronted by everyone and with the utmost urgency. In Australia we should start with biggest source of deceit, and that is the many News Corp outlets; not forgetting the other billionaire-owned far-right media. We've seen the harm the lies from Fox News have done to America's democracy in supporting Trump's lie that he won the 2020 US presidential election and backing him to win again in 2024, so we must stop Murdoch's Sky News and others from doing something similar here. News Corp outlets work very hard at being the propaganda wing of the far-Right. Their reach and power has steadily grown over decades. As a result Australian political opinion is dominated by the News Corp-L/NP partnership. That's been the case for more than 50 years. A prime example of its influence was Murdoch's role in both the election of the Whitlam government in 1972, and in its dismissal in 1975. We are not going to get our democracy back until News Corp stops telling Australians what to think.

No one has all the answers – we must work together and apply critical reasoning. Detailed fact-checking, careful analysis and a commitment to evidence-based truth must be restored to every communications medium so we can all move together in solving problems with minimal division. (No 'alternative facts', please!) Criticism of the RBA and our economics may seem a trivial gripe in the face of our forthcoming extinction, but its neoliberal economics is key to all the economic, political, and cultural reasons behind the dire inadequacy of our response to global heating and the dying biosphere.

Our challenges include the following: the problem of our pollution causing ecological destruction; how our polluting is made worse by our ever-growing linear economy of extraction, production, consumption, and waste; how that is being accelerated by our economics of greed-capitalism and perpetual exponential (percentage) growth; how our many Culturally Acquired Maladaptive Behaviours (especially militarism) have locked us into causing the planet's sixth mass extinction; and how our cultural delusions (notably in economics) are tying us to the unsustainable, destructive, 'Great Acceleration'. I'm trying to say look, there is a comprehensive and cohesive thesis here. All our econo-cultural challenges are why #WorldPeaceNow is vital to this project for survival – we must turn all our resources to responding to these greatest-ever threats – before we are no longer able to.

THE ANALOGY

It was obvious decades ago that our economic system of 'greed & growth capitalism' was causing much of Nature to become a dead wasteland, but what could replace it? The tough question was what might stand a chance of working where so many other systems had more or less failed? Capitalism, communism, and other systems, had failed to deliver a truly fair, kind, egalitarian, open, peaceful, Nature-friendly, science-literate, and sustainable society. So to make civilization sustainable, the focus has to be on both economics and ecology, at their intersection, and how they operate on Spaceship Earth. One insight was that a healthy economic entity operates like a mammalian body, and vice versa, so a body can be an informative analogy (albeit with some limitations) to explain how an economy ought to work.

In this analogy, a body functions in order to serve all its cells (people) fairly. It requires myriad self-adjusting, feed-back regulatory systems to do this, along with vital oversight from a very complicated brain (or government) that incorporates highly effective both central and peripheral nervous (communication) systems. Importantly, a body grows up to its optimum size and then stops growing; this should happen to all national economies.

This analogy gives us a model for a decentralised egalitarian democracy that fairly allocates resources in a way in which greed-capitalism is failing to do. Fairness is a central theme of these ideas, and this includes international climate-justice as well as local social-justice.

The analogy to a living body is consistent with the notion of a circular economy. It is also consistent with being a shrinkable economy and a sustainable, steady-state economy. Others have seen a parallelism between a human body and a national economy, but they saw the corporeal model in a much more negative light. This idea should *not* be confused with *corporatism*. It goes much further by advocating strict worker-ownership of most private enterprises. Briefly stated, the aim is fairness and rule-by-the-people at all levels of society. The aim of economics should not be about productivity and a growing *quantity* of GDP for the benefit of profiteers, but instead improving the genuine *quality* of life for everyone.

THE ADVANTAGE OF PRIVILEGE

Our present system is heavily weighted in favour of those who are previously privileged – that's to say, wealth begets wealth. This can be explained by Games Theory and probability maths, but it's also intuitively obvious that **the more you have, the more you *can* have**. This feature of our system means that rich people will most likely become richer – they can hardly avoid it. Unless factors exist or existed to alter this, then the movement of wealth was *never* a 'trickle-down', it was *always* a 'river-up'. The corollary to that is: **the less you have, the *less* you can have**. Poverty, like profiting, is a self-stoking spiral, and the poor are mathematically most likely to spiral deeper into the inescapable prison of poverty. Poverty is a political choice of voters and governments. (Government please note: Australia's needlessly poor 'Jobseeker' allowance is simply cruel.)

One definition of poverty is that it is the deprivation of all financial and social liberty. If you value personal freedom, consider this: poverty leaves people no freedom to choose anything; it is a loss of liberty second only to detention/jail. Added to that, in our society, it is proportionately more expensive to live if you are poor than if you are rich. Now, in a living body there are many feed-back systems which keep everything in balance, where resources are fed back to needy cells if the fat is building up too much in one spot (as in our rich folk's super-yachts and private jets), but without similarly adequate regulating mechanisms in an economy, then inequality and unfairness inevitably grow. That's the inequality-magnifying world that Neoliberal economics has created and will continue to create until we radically reform it in favour of our survival.

As an aside, in this text I am using the terms right-wing and left-wing. These originated in the French parliament of 1789 when the workers/revolutionaries sat to the left of the presiding officer and the rich aristocrats sat to the right. I use these terms as a generalisation where right-wing means those who desire power and money for themselves, while left-wing means those who desire fairness and well-being for all the people. To put that in slogan-size, the Left wants kindness for all, the Right wants money for the few.

> https://www.history.com/news/how-did-the-political-labels-left-wing-and-right-wing-originate

You'll hear people like Trump and spokes-folks for Murdoch's News Corp complain how terrible 'the Left' is, but they don't dare define what they mean. I've heard ill-informed people say the Nazis were left-wing, which is outrageously untrue. The Nazis calling themselves National Socialists was just to disguise the fact that they were murder-loving anti-human extremists. Euphemisms for themselves and terms of abuse for those they dislike, accusing opponents of their very own crimes, and manipulating language for their own purposes (Orwell's Newspeak) is stock-in-trade for today's neo-Fascists. The term 'woke' is an African-American word meaning awake to veiled racism. Trumpists and the far-Right in the US have stolen the term to use pejoratively against normal people who understand complexity and are comfortable with diversity. The notion of a 'woke agenda' is a nonsense imagined up by the macho simpletons of the Right who fear any sign of cultural difference, science-literacy, or egalitarian compassion. Their so-called woke agenda doesn't exist. L/NP leader Dutton has imported the Trumpist hate-speech tropes because he is too witless to offer any constructive vision of his own. If the one-time workers' party (Labor) wants to retain government then instead of avoiding 'culture conflict' the ALP must find the courage to face down all that Trumpism and nonsense about a non-existent 'woke agenda', to face down all the News Corp deceivers, and to face down all the belligerent, militarist, white-supremacist, 'Christian Nationalist', and American exceptionalism that's coming as an endlessly flooding tsunami-of-insanity from the United States. Of course there are many millions of brilliant, sensible, peace-loving and kind Americans, but some of what's said and done by Americans is unbelievable. The actions, and beliefs of some Americans we see on Australian TV are why I'm frequently heard to exclaim in perplexed frustration and anger: "The Yanks are CRAZY!!!" The re-election of Trump was one of those occasions.

The far-Right say climate science is 'woke', but that just shows their deliberate ignorance. Sadly, governments are punishing climate protesters and accusing them of 'alarmism'. Learning some science of climate change is not 'woke', it is simply NOT being anti-education or anti-reason. Dutton, News Corp and their combined crew of science-denying, pro-nuclear-science (irony there) buffoons may have underestimated the IQ and EQ of Australians. Hopefully, Australians will reject them at every polling booth in favour of wise, well-intentioned, science-literate, independent representatives (such as Senator David Pocock and many others on the current federal cross-benches).

Many of my friends get information from Murdoch's corporation, but they should know that News Corp is just the propaganda machine of the far-right. News Corp supported the Tories in Britain; Fox News promoted Trump in the US, and the many News Corp outlets in Australia almost always support far-right views – many of which are completely detached from reality. Examples include denying that Australians are racist when the evidence is clear that many still are; plus denying that global heating is a threat when it's increasingly obvious that it is, and of course promoting the maladaptive, right-wing folly of economics-for-the-rich, which is our current economic orthodoxy.

SOME HISTORY OF ECONOMICS IS NEEDED

This is because the economists and politicians who follow today's orthodoxy act as if it has all the authority of Holy writ, but it doesn't. Like the popular game of Monopoly (originally called *The Landlord's Game*), the whole game changes if you change the rules of play. The neoliberals never question their dogma about the current set of rules. Yet how we run our economy is neither settled nor sane. For example, it's crazy that the RBA forces mortgage holders to pay twice as much to the banks (in interest) in the name of slowing price-hikes in the supermarkets, yet that's the cruel result of their thirteen interest-rate hikes (so far), and it simply doesn't work! Inflation may eventually slow as unemployment rises under higher interest-rates, but this is a correlation, not causation. Meanwhile the rich get richer and cause demand-pull inflation. The Japanese government and the Bank of Japan has not been so stupid (up until early August 2024 at least), as explained here by Alan Kohler:

> https://www.thenewdaily.com.au/opinion/2023/12/04/alan-kohler-japans-happy-economics

Other examples of our crazy economics include tax cuts for the rich and state governments unable to fund health and education well enough while our federal government holds all the tax powers *and* the power to create as much of our currency as we need. So, for such a currency-issuing government, with that much fiscal power, to deliberately maintain poverty via inadequate welfare is simply heinous! It should be remembered that all welfare money gets spent by needy welfare recipients, and it circulates back to the wealthy business owners and creates demand for basic goods and services like food, education and health care. Then this same money can be returned to the government via the taxes it collects from rich individuals and the rich corporations such as Coles, Woolworths and others. So welfare payments and pensions are not inflationary because the poor have limited purchasing power and do not chase prices up – *aka* do not create demand-pull inflation. Rather, welfare is essential for keeping the lower-reaches of the national economy both alive and well. Further to that, to needlessly chase non-existent debts via the illegal Robodebt scam was no more than a way to punch down on the less fortunate. Sadly, that cruelty drove many to suicide. And the recent Robotax raiding is almost as bad. Worst of all is that this powerful politico-economic institution we call our government is acting as if building a war-economy is the top priority of the nation. For example, the insane and insanely expensive AUKUS agreement is all about helping America make war – while many Australians remain deprived of health, a home, or even enough food.

George Monbiot is right when he says we need to know what capitalism is before we can change it to a better system. What is capitalism? An abbreviated and elaborated version of the definition from Investopedia is this: **Capitalism** is an economic system in which private individuals or businesses own capital. Capital is productive equipment, or property, or the cash to buy a share in such productive capacity. (So in turn businesses may be owned by sharebludgers like me.) The capital is used to exploit a resource for the purpose of profit. Labour doesn't own the means of production but instead uses the means of production to make profits for the benefit of the owners of capital. The production of goods and services under capitalism is based on a market economy. This is in contrast to a planned economy or a command economy. One form of capitalism is neoliberal, free-market, or laissez-faire capitalism. In that system private profiteering individuals are restrained as little as possible. The owners decide where to invest, what to produce or sell, and at which prices to exchange goods and services. The idealized laissez-faire marketplace would operate without checks or controls. Today, most countries practice a mixed capitalist system that includes some degree of government regulation of businesses, and some degree of public ownership.

Now we've got a description of capitalism I'll go on to briefly describe how we got the present economic orthodoxy called neoliberalism. But while we are considering any redesign of the system, we should consider what's foundational to civil society, and then work from there. Obviously we need to keep the 'trade in goods and services' part of our economic system, but as the Monopoly game showed, it's the rules of the game that makes all the difference. Neoliberal economics invented a set of rules that favoured the rich and did its best to emasculate democracy and social well-being. Monbiot says there is no good versus bad capitalism; it's all bad because capital always exploits wealth for the profit of the oligarchs and creates inequality and economic injustice for workers. (So maybe a better system needs a new name, but lacking one now, I'd say that's the least of our worries.)

Increasingly, people are seeing how neoliberal, free-market economics has been a cruel, deceitful, and global disaster ever since it became the strictly-exclusive economics dogma four decades ago. **Neoliberalism** brought in an ethos devoted to making a killing as opposed to making a living. (That's ironic as we face extinction!) For those who're not students of economics, there are, broadly speaking, two contesting schools within the discipline (with many sub-sects), namely Keynesian and Neoliberal economics. Liberalism, the senior school, comes from European Neoclassical economists of the 18th and 19th centuries.

We can't discuss economics without mentioning the Scotsman, Adam Smith (1723–1790) who wrote *The Theory of Moral Sentiments* (1759) and *An Inquiry into the Nature and Causes of the Wealth of Nations* (1776). Among many other ideas, Smith is credited with the idea of the 'invisible hand' of the market, but he also thought market economics should operate within a reasonably compassionate society, and his *homo economicus* is a moral person. The many others who contributed to economic thought are too numerous to mention.

Neoliberalism got its name because its 20th century proponents admired aspects of liberal thought that came out of the European Enlightenment. A core value of liberalism is personal liberty, but the zeitgeist of capitalism from the 1980s onwards ('greed is good') was to overreach on the pursuit of individual freedom at the expense of fairness, collective action, democratic governance, and egalitarian social-well-being. The liberalism that holds the individual to be sacrosanct rejects the fact that everything we achieve as humans, from a match-box to a moon-shot, is a product of co-operation and collective effort. (See the 2011 book *Super Cooperators* by Martin Nowak and Roger Highfield) The men driving that old economics favoured unregulated markets and a laissez-faire (literally, 'allow-to-do'), profit-motivated capitalism.

Today's idolatry of the myth of the 'free market' arose back when most people were primitive enough to believe in an omnipotent deity. So the patriarchal, invisible, omniscient, righteous-power of Smith's 'invisible hand' seemed to justify their abrogation of responsibility for their fellow humans. It suited the wealth-seeking industrialists of the industrial revolution, and the free-market suited the entrepreneurs of the British Empire.

Through a long line of laissez-faire ideologues and dedicated neo-aristocrats, including Ludwig von Mises (1881–1973), Friedrich Hayek (1899–1992), Rose Friedman (1910–2009) and Milton Friedman (1912–2006), and other members of the Mont Pelerin Society (a conservative group founded in 1947), the economic-fundamentalist faith in individual rights, free enterprise, and competition was revived and came to dominate the late 20th century. These economists were proudly anti-egalitarian and opposed to any principle of fairness. They shamelessly asserted that economic injustice and social inequality were good and right (some even believed inequality was ordained by their god). They feared the rule of 'King mob' – as they saw democracy – and correctly feared the centralisation of power and possession as exemplified by Stalinist communism. But the democratic counter-view asserts that the well-being of each individual grows out of a harmonious and egalitarian society which nurtures *every* member of society, or community, not just privileging a few. Egalitarian democracy means individual liberty arising from *within* the co-operative mob, rather than liberty imposed legally (and perhaps violently) from *outside* the feared mob by an authoritarian state, dictator, or oligarchy. An egalitarian will emphasize universal human rights, whereas a libertarian will emphasize personal property rights. Many people mistakenly think that *egalitarian* means everyone is identical. Egalitarian does mean *equal* in the sense of equal rights, but it also means *similarity* and may be better interpreted as fairness or social justice. Neoliberal capitalism is ideologically opposed to fairness. It favours inequality and is designed to help the rich to get richer. Neoliberalism is opposed to any fair social-democracy, and evidence shows that the ultra-rich and billionaires are powerfully opposed to democracy itself. From the 1980s onward the world embraced this right-wing, classist ideology – especially due to support from Margaret Thatcher and Ronald Reagan.

There's a long history to how denial of climate science has overlapped with neoliberalism, and how climate action became a victim of the free-market absolutists, capitalist economists, and politicians. It's well summarised in this 45 minute video by Simon Clark: *The Decade We Lost the Planet* (or how politico-economic ideology killed the science):

https://www.youtube.com/watch?v=hvGQMZFP9IA

Adding to the above, in a 1970 essay by Milton Friedman in *The New York Times* entitled "A Friedman doctrine – The Social Responsibility of Business Is to Increase Its Profits", Friedman defied reality by specifically rejecting the notion that business was part of society or had any responsibility to society. He said that any business with a 'social conscience' and which *takes seriously its responsibilities for providing employment, eliminating discrimination,* [and] *avoiding pollution* was *undermining the basis of a free society*. His attitude, and that of his supporters was anti-human and anti-Nature. This attitude of 'profit-first, people and the planet last' has prevailed for decades. That mind-set is what we must vigorously reject and rise above. To Friedman and his supporters, the only job of business was profit, by fair means or foul. For too long we've had mostly foul.

The neoliberal ideology included the idea of 'shareholder value'. This was the corollary of the profit-at-all-costs doctrine, whereby the owners of companies, the shareholders, were entitled to have the return on their investments maximised. Still we hear right-wing pundits insisting on ever-increasing productivity (getting more profit for less cost), and for guaranteed 'shareholder value'. There's an epithet for unemployed people that was popular among those whose income was secure, and that was 'dole-bludger'. To reflect this back on the many shareholders who are living off unearned income, the term 'share-bludger' can be coined. While-ever we idle share-bludgers are the most privileged people in our society we are not going to build a sustainable economy nor prevent ecological breakdown.

In his 1962 book *Capitalism and Freedom*, Milton Friedman compared liberalism and egalitarianism, asserting that social justice is not compatible with being a (neo) liberal. He had no idea of the 'river-up' flow (*not* 'trickle-down') of money in capitalism, and of the river-up effect of pre-existing wealth and privilege. Friedman and that ideological school actually wanted to legitimize *plutocracy*: government by the rich, for the rich. Their instinct was to re-establish an aristocracy of the *nouveau riche*, a structure of wealth, power and entitlement that had existed in Europe and was mimicked in America's Gilded Age (as Mark Twain called it) when in the late 1800s there was great inequality, a river-up flow of wealth, plus broad corruption, which is with us again. Conversely, a government that facilitates economic justice is simply putting fairness into action. As said, care is love in action. If we have the heart to want to live in a fair and caring society, and to love one another (John 13:34), then we should happily support the correcting flow of redistribution.

Economic justice and fairness are not among the values of neoliberalism. Rather our present economics is home to cynicism and selfishness – as the Robodebt scandal showed. (See Rick Morton's 2024 book, *Mean Streak*.) A major question for politicians, economists and philosophers is: how can we all live well? The response of neoliberal capitalism has been just, 'Be greedy!' Sadly, a line derived from Oliver Stone's 1987 movie *Wall Street*, 'Greed is good' became the mantra of the neoliberal project of the moneyed elites that have been running the world over recent decades. In the film, Gordon Gekko, the character played by Michael Douglas, gives a speech on what he perceives as the virtues of greed. The speech was meant to be ironic, and the whole film was meant to be a morality tale on the dangers of lying, greedy, selfish competition, but many people took it as a guide-book instead.

People who work in agriculture, and are exposed to the elements and other animals, know that Nature shows us repeatedly that when it comes to how we can all live well, then selfish greed leads to violence towards one another, and is exactly wrong. We need honest sharing, and the non-violence of caring co-operation, if we are to survive.

KEYNESIANISM

The younger yet more important school of capitalist economics (notice we are not even considering the econo-politics of either Engels/Marxism or Lenin/Stalinism here), is that which arose from John Maynard Keynes (1883–1946) and was the dominant school of economic thinking for roughly forty years from 1939 to 1979. Keynes's influence was, and remains, enormous. Not only did he influence many economists and politicians, but his ideas sat well with those governments of the era that were inclined to take responsibility for the progress and well-being of their citizens; not merely to justify their own re-election, but also to try to prevent the sort of suffering that occurred during the Great Depression and to aid the recovery of nations devastated by the wars. It should be remembered that Keynes was trying to save British capitalism from its own crushing classism and from what was, in the early part of the 20th century, the appeal and popularity of communism. While Keynes could hardly be called a socialist, his insights enabled many countries to achieve a more kindly form of democratic socialism for which the Nordic countries are still well known today. See George Lakey's 2017 book, *Viking Economics*. The self-titled Modern Monetary Theory (MMT) is an economic model that, in part, grew out of Keynesianism.

Although the many threads of economic thinking are mind-boggling to non-economists like me, the chief difference between the two schools is that Friedmanites think free competition in unregulated markets provides a reliable 'invisible hand' and that all society's requirements should be left to the markets and the profiteers to allocate without any external intervention. Meanwhile Keynesians tend to the opinion that there is no truly free market, that markets often fail, that competition is rarely perfect, that the creaming-off of profits from privatised services does not provide the greatest good for the greatest number, and that therefore it's the responsibility of all democratically elected governments to re-allocate resources so that society's requirements are met much more efficiently and fairly.

Ever since the rise of the monetarist/neoliberal school, which was championed by Reagan and Thatcher, there's been an argument going on between the devotees of laissez-faire and those who believe governments should be responsible for the society they were elected to govern. Young people today do not remember that for much of the 20th century governments at least *tried* to act in the best interests of their people and that a democratic and egalitarian society is both possible and desirable. The young have been enculturated to see governments and politicians as the cynical, self-serving and deceitful servants of corporations and of the plutocrat/oligarchs who run big-business. That's sad, but it doesn't have to be this way.

The views of Keynes and his supporters held sway until neoliberalism took over in the early 1980s. Any history of modern economics must include the on-going consequences of the 1944 Bretton Woods conference, which made the US dollar the world's reserve currency, plus the boost the WWII 'war-economy' gave to America and which that nation and its Military-Industrial-Complex has continued through perpetual war ever since. At the same time, the dark art of predatory lending and placing poorer countries in debt traps (for infrastructure projects) was perfected by the US (via USAID and the CIA) and the International Monetary Fund (IMF). This was well described in John Perkins' book, *Confessions of an Economic Hit-Man*, first published in 2004 and re-published in 2016. No American should accuse China of creating debt traps without great embarrassment. And it must be noted that America's security/military agencies, such as the CIA, have a long history of interfering in other countries for the perceived economic benefit of the US.

Returning to the history of **neoliberalism**, its ideologues took a long look at the 10-point plan of economist John Williamson (and others), who was based in Washington, and they thought, 'We can use this', then they added their own extras. Williamson's plan included:

1 fiscal discipline to keep deficit spending low compared to GDP
2 redirecting public money away from subsidies and towards public services like health and education
3 tax reform to broaden the tax base (consumption taxes) and moderate income taxes
4 interest rates that are determined largely by money markets (US Dollar dominated)
5 floating international currency exchange rates determined by (US dominated) money markets only
6 free trade between countries as far as diverse nations will tolerate – i.e. tariff-barrier breakdown
7 allowing foreign investment to enter countries freely to exploit their labour and resources
8 privatization of all government-owned enterprises, assets and public services
9 abolition of all regulations that might hinder foreign investors (*aka* raider/privateers)
10 secure legal property rights for foreign companies seeking to exploit subordinate nations.

However, the neoliberals took away item 2 completely and added in their own:

1. Monetarism – the idea that interest rates alone determine the money supply and the rate of inflation
2. the maintenance of a constant level of inflation advantaging businesses and disadvantaging customers
3. NAIRU – a scheme for maintaining a cruelly high number of unemployed to stop wage demands
4. supply-side economics – i.e. profiteering via ever-growing production, flogging-stuff, and trashing it
5. minimal taxes for the rich – pressuring impotent governments to let the rich get richer
6. minimal government – i.e. crippling governments so they can't regulate anyone or nationalise anything.

The neoliberal project became conflated with Williamson's original plan and was called the **Washington Consensus**. This ideology, especially its demands for impotent governments, deregulation, the free movement of raider-capital, and privatising everything, enabled the 'greed is good' pirates to take over almost every country in the world. Sadly, the Hawke and Keating governments in Australia were convinced to adopt this form of economics, and the Labor party of today, under Treasurer Chalmers, is fully committed to this idiotic, oligarch-enriching form of economics. (Much to the delight of Mr. Dutton and his good friend Gina Reinhart.) We see neoliberal economics in the gutting of the public service and in the well-established crony-corruption between governments, lobbyists, consultants (PWC *et al*), and corporations (e.g. Santos, Woodside, and all the other extraction corporations taking super profits out of Australia). We see it in the aged-care sector where our elders are fed on $6 a day so the privateers can live in mansions. And we see it in the largely foreign-owned banks taking record profits overseas.

It should be noted that working-class Americans and many Australians, plus most of our politicians, have been conned into thinking that the oligarchs, and the economic system that enriches them, will enrich us too. Many people have also been induced to believe that a successful, peaceful country like China is going to enslave them while all the time it is neoliberal capitalism that actually enslaves and impoverishes them.

It's worth quoting verbatim one of the things Investopedia says about capitalism: *The purest form of capitalism is free-market or laissez-faire capitalism. Here, private individuals are unrestrained.* That's to say, under this 'pure' form of capitalism there is no regulation of individual privateers. But it's simply not true that neoliberal economists believed in total deregulation. Neoliberal economists just wanted one set of regulations, but not another. They wanted tax cuts for the rich; property rights for the rich; free movement of capital and profit so that exploitation and its takings could cross all borders; they wanted the weakest governments possible because strong governments might be democratic and assert the will of the underprivileged; they wanted institutional inflation to provide a permanent advantage for price-setters over price-takers. And the neoliberals wanted little or no union membership so they had compliant workers. They wanted share ownership so the rich could be remote owners and receive unearned income; plus they wanted preferential treatment for landlords. They had lobbyists to tell governments what to do, and consulting firms to take lots of public money to help the lobbyists erase democracy from the halls of that pro-business regulation institution, formerly known as our parliament. Most importantly the libertarian neoliberals demanded the regulation that's called 'no environmental regulation' so they could exploit Nature and pollute as much as they liked and have no consequences – privatize the profits and nationalise/socialise the loss and damage. That's what the fossil fuel industry has been doing for decades. Basically, the neoliberal economists wanted deregulation for the rich and the capitalists, but regulation on the poor to keep minimum wages as low as possible. Plus they wanted a finance sector for the financiers, floating currencies for the money marketeers, and a huge games advantage for the American dollar as the World's reserve currency. Also, let's not forget that neoliberalism was largely an American invention.

Thankfully, there is a movement against neoliberal capitalism, and more people are demanding that governments once again take responsibility for social well-being. Many people have raged against greed-capitalism, but few have forced change in the way things are done or managed to keep hard-right capitalists out of political power. Neoliberalism convinced governments that if they ensured rich people were getting richer then this would automatically make everything fine in the world. That's nonsense, of course. Along with its demands for tax cuts and radical privatisation, the advocates of market fundamentalism convinced a lot of people that 'the market' should be 'set free' to provide for everyone's needs. Added to that, people actually believed the idiotic idea that if the rich could keep getting richer then some of those riches would 'trickle down'. This idea had been ridiculed a century ago, but many people still believed it. Many others saw that it was always lies and bulldust. Small-government ideology aims to disempower our elected representatives and replace democratic governments with rule by the rich (plutocracy), rule by the ultra-rich (oligarchy) or rule by the corporations (corporatocracy), which is why our centres of power are flooded with rent-seeking lobbyists, and why most public services have been outsourced to overpaid 'consultants'. Neoliberal capitalism was always and everywhere about exploiting everything for the benefit of the rich.

MONETARISM

I'm sorry, this gets unavoidably technical, but it's because we have to change the whole system and everyone needs to know enough economics so they can help make that happen. Monetarism is one part of the overall neoliberal-Friedmanite economic ideology, and, as its name suggests, it's about the governance of our money. The website Investopedia has the most accessible explanations, so I'll paraphrase from there. Monetarism is a dogma based on a theory that says governments can support economic stability by affecting changes in the money supply. (If they really believed that, then monetarists would adjust up and down their taxes on the rich – where the bulk of the public's money goes to – but instead they adjust the price of money, i.e. interest rates, because that suits the plutocracy much better.) Monetarists believe that increases in the supply of money causes inflation (price rises of any rate), but it's not so. Prices don't rise by themselves. Inflation is caused by price-setters putting up their prices – either because they have to, or just because they want to.

Monetarist theory centres on a formula called 'the quantity theory of money' which states that the money supply multiplied by its velocity (the rate at which money changes hands) is equal to expenditures (goods and services) multiplied by price. The equation is expressed as $MV=PQ$ where: M=the money supply, multiplied by V=velocity (the rate at which money is spent annually), equals P=the average price of a good or service, multiplied by Q=the quantity of goods and services sold. **Put simply, the idea is that money circulates with the same speed and quantity as economic activity requires it to.** Duh! How could it be otherwise? Where economists differ is that monetarists say the money supply controls economic activity while others say economic activity determines the money supply. But that's the thing about equations, they work both ways, so $PQ=MV$ as well. In practice it means that monetarists focus on only interest rates as an economic lever, while Keynesians focus on the demand that drives economic activity.

In their 1963 book, *A Monetary History of The United States, 1867–1960* Milton Friedman and Anna Jacobson Schwartz argued in favour of monetarism as a way to combat the negative effects of inflation, but the truth is that monetarists actually welcome some inflation. (There's a reason the RBA likes a 2–3% annual inflation rate.) The so-called K-Percent Rule was an idea by Friedman that central banks should increase the money supply every year by a rate equal to the growth of gross domestic product (GDP). So, embedded in this is the notion of perpetual economic growth and perpetual loss of purchasing power for workers (plus the less-than full employment myth of NAIRU); and these are assumed as a matter of course. We will revisit this fact, that economic growth is no more than an **un**examined assumption.

While Friedman and friends assumed GDP could grow forever, economists such as Ernst Schumacher and Kenneth Boulding (both heroes of sustainability, wisdom, and peace) knew that infinite growth on a finite planet was absurd. E. F. Schumacher wrote:

> *An entirely new system of thought is needed, a system based on attention to people, and not primarily attention to goods ...*

and also wrote:

> *Anyone who thinks consumption can expand forever on a finite planet is either insane or an economist.*

And in reference to fossil fuels he pointed out that our civilization is living on irreplaceable capital while greedily treating it as income. Another advocate of sustainable living, Kenneth E. Boulding wrote, *Anyone who believes in indefinite growth in anything physical, on a physically finite planet, is either mad or an economist.* And yes, both were economists.

What Australians need to know is that all our federal Treasurers, their bureaucrats, and our Reserve Bank, are all monetarists; they believe in perpetual economic growth and in perpetually increasing productivity (getting more out for less input) of the workforce despite the fact that we live in a finite ecosystem and that productivity *must* tend to a limit.

Apologies again, but we need a couple more descriptions of terms. Two explanations needed here are monetary and fiscal policy. **Monetary policy** is primarily interest rate control. More broadly it's the set of methods Reserve Banks use to supposedly control the money supply, by changing the RBA's national base interest rate but also by tinkering with the rules that the bank applies to the private banks. In Australia, the Treasury does *not* (as stated above) change tax rates to control the money supply (governments are too afraid of the political backlash). This makes the RBA relatively ineffectual because they only have interest rates to make noticeable change in the economy. Also, the RBA doesn't care much if the money supply is poorly controlled as long as the supply is rising, because that means the numbers are growing in rich people's savings accounts. Plus, it adds to the appearance of economic growth, and reduces the purchasing power of workers' wages – so all good for business owners and plutocrats.

Fiscal policy is mostly government spending. (Reference: Investopedia) It *does* include adjusting taxation policies, but, because these policies change so slowly (due to political pressures) and because neoliberalism continually demands lower taxes on the rich, taxation is an economic lever that our federal government rarely touches and only then with great trepidation. Fiscal policy is still somewhat influenced by Keynesian economics because Keynes recognised that governments were a sufficiently large economic player that the timing and volume of spending interventions could moderate fluctuations in what they call the 'business cycle' rather than leave it to the markets (a bit like using IV fluids to stabilise a patient's cardio-vascular homeostasis), but Keynesianism is unpopular today.

Socially empathic folks suggest that the federal government *should* be deploying spending and taxation to direct resources for the good of society (like boosting health and aged care, building public housing, and funding all levels of education properly), but successive governments have been afraid of doing this for fear of being accused of socialism (as if socialism is actually bad). As Richard Denniss has pointed out, Norway taxes its resource sector and provides free universities while Australia subsidises its resource sector and charges huge fees to university students for which most have to go into a compounding HECS debt. Australia's public money that could be going to fund free tertiary education and cancel all HECS debt is instead being funneled into the US war machine via the $368 billion AUKUS scam. If we cancelled AUKUS we could easily make all education totally free, and pay back all HECS contributions that never should have been imposed, let alone indexed to keep growing each year. Denmark, Iceland, Finland and Sweden all offer low cost universities. Our universities could be devoted to education again instead of being business corporations with overpaid CEOs (sorry, Vice Chancellors). Without AUKUS Australia could afford a lot of things that we actually need.

Free education would not be inflationary. As explained elsewhere, what causes inflation depends on where government largess goes. If public money goes to the less privileged it circulates benignly back to the government. But if it's in the form of tax cuts for the rich or higher interest money going to the rich, then that will promote price rises. Some on the Right of politics have exaggerated the effects of government spending and falsely accused Australia's federal government of stoking inflation by spending too much. They are either ignorant or liars; I wonder which.

Federal Government spending is hardly stoking inflation – especially not by comparison with the higher interest and tax cuts going to rich people, or the greedflation of the supermarket duopoly. One of the few times the federal regime has put out expansionary spending was during the peak of Covid – which was fair enough – but there was no inflationary effect until some of that money flowed to the rich. The other big spending that federal governments do is for multinational consultancy firms, billions in fossil fuel subsidies (which must be stopped yesterday) and their seemingly limitless funding of the Australian-American military alliance. Interestingly, building an arms industry and paying huge money to AUKUS is not considered inflationary. That's because that portion of our national coffers gets shipped to America and is never seen again.

Nonetheless, conservatives still argue falsely that government spending is to blame for inflation. They are dogmatic that the money supply, rather than consumer demand, is what drives price rises. Which brings us to another dispute between Neoliberal economics and Keynesian economics. This is over **supply-side** versus **demand-side** theories. In short, the neoliberal Friedmanites say that increasing the *supply* of goods and services will drive economic growth – a sort of 'make it and they will buy' mindset – whereas Keynesians say the driver of economic activity is the *demand* for goods and services. In other words, if enough people want something, and if they can pay for it, then someone will get to work to provide it. You decide which makes more sense.

The two terms became synonymous with their respective doctrines. So 'demand-side economics' is another name for Keynesianism and 'supply-side economics' means Friedmanism. Friedman's supply-side doctrines acquired other names as well, often determined by who was championing them: Reaganomics in the US; Thatcherism in the UK; Rogernomics in New Zealand (after Roger Douglas). The term 'economic rationalism' was used in Australia while names used elsewhere included the Washington Consensus and Monetarism, as described above. As also mentioned, the Friedmanite doctrine advocated tax cuts for the rich and promoted the idiotic and arrogant notion that wealth could trickle down to the poor. It was a 'crumbs from my table', nouveau-feudalist attitude. Reagan deployed the silly analogy of 'a rising tide lifts all boats' to justify the doctrine (and political 'justification by growth' still persists), but capitalism was never like that. Rather, the rising tide of worker-generated productivity tended to lift the more expensive yachts the most, but left the worker's dinghies stuck in the mud. To paraphrase a saying by John Maynard Keynes: [free market] *capitalism is the astounding belief that the worst people will do the worst things for the greatest good of everyone.*

There's plenty to criticise about neoliberal economics and the neo-aristocratic values and attitudes of its ideological midwives, the Friedmans, Hayek, and others from the Mont Pelerin Society, but what exemplifies it very clearly is its fanatical drive to *privatisation*. Putting the supply of goods and services in the hands of privateers shifts the goal of enterprise onto the job of *raking-in-money* in place of the goal of ***doing a care-full job***. But care is love in action, and if we are to heal Nature and civil society, then they need all the love we can give. (Did you know the etymology of *cure* is from the Latin *cura* meaning care? I mean to hint that if we are going to cure the world's problems then we all need to care.)

PRIVATISATION

Privatisation leads to rising inequality and poorer outcomes everywhere. Making our lives all about money incentivises corruption so corruption is what we get. Neoliberal economics, greed and growth economics, has tried to privatise everything that looked like it might have a profit in it:

a 'business model' for the privateers. If the term 'privateers' evokes the pirates of the 1700s it's because extreme-capitalists *are* pirates and slavers. Theft by legal means is still theft. Profiteering breeds carelessness. It's why private aged care facilities had the poorest food, the poorest client care, and the highest Covid deaths. Privatisation is behind the chronic **ambulance ramping** in Australia because there hasn't been enough public money put into creating enough aged-care and hospital beds. Neoliberal economics *reduced* the number of hospital beds and sacked as many health-care workers as possible despite our growing population. (I saw this as a registered nurse in 1993. An 'economic rationalist' bureaucrat outsourced the catering at my hospital and sacked 40% of the catering staff. Nursing staff were scarce too. Morale was at rock bottom. Coincidently our politicians voted themselves a 40% pay rise at the same time. This sparked my interest in economics.)

Plus, the economic rationalists shut the 'convalescent hospitals', abolished step-down units and minimised community care. So now hospitals all over Australia suffer 'bed-block' where people who are too unwell for discharge prevent people being admitted quickly from emergency departments, and acute cases have to wait outside in Ambulances that should be performing timely urgent care. The problems of EDs have always been about flow-through – they need hydrodynamics specialists, not MBA 'managers'.

New South Wales, Queensland and Victoria all suffer from those public-pays-twice privatised toll roads that are great cash-cows for the companies that own them. Private profit was why Australia's disability scheme (NDIS) was outrageously rorted by the privateers.

The Australian government used to provide reliable and affordable services through publicly owned institutions such as banking via the Commonwealth Bank, communications originally via the PMG and then Telecom, regional air transport via TAA and international flights via QANTAS, employment services via the CES, and many more. Now all these services have been privatised to the detriment of all except the profiteering owners. The private companies are competing madly for profit, cutting each other down, cutting services and sacking as many people as they can. The result is that Australians have much poorer services that cost a lot more and which employ many fewer of us. And all just for profit.

Profiteering has become a national and global sport, and the game-players revel in it. Right-wing folks like to repeat the myth that the private sector can provide services more efficiently than the public sector, but, all management etc being equal, private sector services will always be more expensive (and therefore less efficient) than public services because the privateers have to cream off their profits – which a public service doesn't have to generate. The profit motive is partly why Medicare has been neglected and health care in Australia has again become a two-tiered system: one for the wealthy and one for the rest. Private profiteering is behind the paucity of all our services. It is behind the high cost of living, and private profiteering puts significant restraint on climate action.

Profiteering is why flight-safety is trending backwards. It's behind Boeing's problems. It's why fossil fuel corporations are careless of everything that might slow their profiteering and why they get our law-enforcers to jail environment defenders and climate change protesters. It's why extractivist companies have committed resource-theft everywhere. It's why transnational corporations have exploited labour in nations like China and India and why many more countries have the ***wage slavery*** of ultra-low wages and conditions, thereby also abolishing jobs in high-wage nations. Countries like Bangladesh, Malaysia, and Vietnam come to mind. Critically, if we are ever to live well again, we must abandon the motive of greed/profit and put the motive of *care* permanently in its place.

As I see it, one of the defining characteristics of neoliberal capitalism is its lack of care. It is geared to exploit the Earth and people without remorse. Friedman specifically stated that considerations of workers and the environment were to be ignored by business, which only had a duty to maximise profit. However, the alternative to neoliberal greed-capitalism is not communism, it is democracy – government of the people, by the people, and FOR the people – plus workers genuinely owning the means of production via worker-ownership cooperatives and other democratic structures. The whole world has to decide whether we want our governments (the state) to *care for* everyone or just pamper the rich. If it's to be everyone, then we have to make companies stop their ruthless profiteering, end their careless, biosphere-destroying extracting, exploiting and polluting, and stop them carelessly gouging prices up. Plus, we have to overthrow the deity of 'the market' and fully reject the profit-motivated religion of marketism.

Since I mentioned them, co-operatives can work really well. The famous Mondragon group of 81 cooperatives employs around 70,000 people in the Basque region of Spain. It began in 1955 when a Catholic priest by the name of José María Arizmendiarrieta selected five young technical school students to establish the first co-operative of the Mondragon Corporation. Arizmendiarrieta spent years teaching people about a form of humanism based on solidarity and participation. These ideals persist in the group to this day. Similarly, the Huawei corporation is also a cooperative. Founded in China in 1987 by Ren Zhengfei, Huawei says it is a global provider of information and communications technology (ICT) equipment with around 207,000 employees operating in 170 countries. So there are numerous successful and worker-friendly alternatives to neoliberal capitalism with its inequality, its ecocidal destruction, labour exploitation, greedflation, and profiteering.

MODERN MONETARY THEORY

One group that's saying "wait a minute" to the neoliberal ideologues is the proponents of Modern Monetary Theory (MMT). There's a big unanswered question for us non-economists, and that is who or what 'creates' our money in Australia? In her 2020 book *The Deficit Myth*, Professor Stephanie Kelton implies that the US monetary system destroys tax dollars, that is, *deletes* the numbers that arrive as revenue at the US tax office. Does Australia's Tax Office do the same, or not? Some supporters of MMT say that Australia's money system *does* work the same as in America, and that it both creates and destroys each nominal dollar in our money supply. This implies that the Australian currency/money does not circulate at all, and that the only point of any taxation is to prevent the quantum of currency in the economy from growing too large. I doubt this is either fully true or ideal, but the point is that the Australian public has not been informed how our money moves. Creation and destruction may be how other countries manage their money supply, but it's not clear how it's managed in Australia – at least not as far as the public understands how our government is supposed to tax and spend. Most of us are deliberately fed the myth that it's only taxpayers who pay for everything, but it isn't so. A quick way to learn how Stephanie Kelton and others re-thought the money-go-round is by watching the documentary film *Finding The Money*, which outlines MMT in the US.

There's a difference between the Australian and US systems that should be noted here. The original United States Federal Reserve Act of 1913 established the US Federal Reserve System (nick-named 'The Fed'), which is a set of twelve regional reserve banks and a central government body in Washington. Where the American Reserve Bank System differs from the Australian Reserve Bank is that the US version is a set of privately owned banks, whereas Australia's RBA is publicly owned and controlled by our government. Although that seems like a big difference, in practice and due to the legal framework that's been built around their system, the US 'Fed' acts for the US government in much the same way as our RBA. Both can buy any debt instruments the government issues (bonds etc) and both can 'create' (often referred to as 'print') the national currency.

Notwithstanding the opacity around the process of money creation in Australia, MMT advocates are correct in pointing out that any government that creates its own currency cannot normally go bankrupt in its own currency. So who creates our money in Australia? Some MMT advocates say it is the Australian Treasury by writing cheques. In 2023, the then RBA governor Lowe said it's only the RBA that creates our money. And in talks given by Professor Richard Werner (on YouTube), he says it is the commercial banks that create the bulk of our money – every time they issue a loan. This is especially so because the commercial banks don't have to draw on their reserves when they issue a loan; they just click a computer mouse to create your home loan (or whatever it's for – either a productive or unproductive purpose). That's to say the banks can lend more than they actually have in their accounts as long as no one calls them out or there is a 'run' on deposits. In other words, private commercial banks are the only sort of profiteering business that is legally allowed to operate while insolvent. And because the private banks are not 100% capitalised (meaning their holdings are smaller than their financial obligations), this is one reason why we see banks 'collapsing', such as the Silicon Valley Bank, and why we see governments rushing in to guarantee that each depositor's 'money' (somewhere on a bank memory chip) won't vanish. This is also why Australia's RBA props up our (largely foreign-owned) commercial banks with ample public money.

In practice it is probably all three institutions that 'create' our money, but that's a detail which needs to be clarified. Certainly, all politicians, treasurers, and finance ministers, brazenly maintain the utter fiction that the federal budget is like a household budget and that tax revenue is essential to their budget. It must be added that with so much money being created, the money supply could be ballooning dangerously, so it's vital for the people's government to get a lot of it back via taxation. This is where taxes do their job of retrieving public money back to our government. Here MMT says that the government (Treasury and the Reserve Bank) and the private banks 'create' the money and taxes 'destroy' the money. That's not literally true because most of our 'money' is only numbers on accounting ledgers, or electrons in a computer chip, so it's only a philosophical debate whether numbers are created or destroyed. Our money only has a material form when there's cash in your wallet. Coins and banknotes only *represent* 'money'.

So, getting back to the true nature of money, it's all just a record of numbers. Money has always been just an accounting tool. For millennia in exchange and trade the money has been a handy way to ensure 'fair exchange, no robbery'. In practice, only damaged coins and notes get physically destroyed and replaced by fresh ones from the Mint, but that doesn't disrupt the ledger-keeping. Ideally the ledgers should show the books are balanced, even if sometimes they are fudged. Which is also why it's nothing but cruel for governments to chase down tiny welfare sums [RoboDebt], tiny tax liabilities [RoboTax], or ridiculously auto-increasing HECS debts that are indexed to inflation – especially when governments are willing to throw $billions at the totally wasteful and useless military sector.

Many bankers (e.g. RBA governor Bullock) and governments don't like cash because cash is money that has escaped from the account ledger for a while and is less easy to keep account of. Authoritarians want to know every little thing we do. In that way, cash is money that's been *liberated* from the clutches of governments and the banks – which is why we rightly feel our liberty is under threat from those who want to make our currency totally digital. And whether the money is figurative on a paper or electronic ledger, or whether it is literal in the form of cash in hand, to do its job the money has to circulate – currency needs to flow. When it stops flowing enough (for whatever reason), then it fails in its service.

MMT advocates are also right in saying that most of us misunderstand the way a currency-issuing government operates. We are led to believe that it starts with taxation (the government's income) and ends with spending in the same way that a household budget does, and that if the income over outgo ratio is less than 1 (one), then this budget deficit is bad in the same way that ours is when we are going broke. That *is* the way state and local governments work, but it *is not* how our federal government works, and a budget deficit for a currency-issuing government is not, in itself, a problem because the feds cannot go broke in our own money. MMT explains that the federal government works in reverse; that it starts by spending and ends with income (tax revenue) because this is how it 'creates' the money supply. This's essentially correct, but it overlooks a few things. Firstly, there has been 'money' in our civilised society for a very long time, so it's more about supply *management* than creation. Secondly, it's the private banks that are adding by far the largest quantity of 'numbers' (dollars) to the money supply. Thirdly, the numbers of dollars are only a rough representation of the actual *value* that's 'created'. So in fact our money supply doesn't have any starting point – circles don't need any start or finish.

I should point out the biggest scam the private banks are running: they literally *make* money. This is why our elected government should **see banking as an essential service** and as a natural monopoly. And it's why governments should nationalise the whole sector for the benefit of all the people (as Ben Chifley proposed). These unelected, almost totally unaccountable, profiteer-pirates (the private banks) literally ***make money*** out of nothing!

As mentioned, each time someone gets a bank loan, the bank just writes (clicks) those numbers into existence (as credit) and then you can go to buy your house (or whatever), and the bank trusts that you will bring the *value* of that credit back in many little packages from your wages as you work towards repaying the loan over the next thirty years (or however long it takes). Getting that loan means that suddenly you've got a liability, and the bank has an asset. The scam of it is that, over that time, and depending on the annual interest rates being charged, you will have paid back much more than the value of the original credit, and that sum could easily end up being twice the *value* of the original loan. You will pay very dearly for the bank to realise its asset. So the rich owners of the private bank may end up with two 'houses-worth' that your work has created the value of, but *you* only get one. It's called *usury*, and some people throughout history have banned it.

Returning to the purpose of taxation, many have rightly suggested that adjusting tax rates up or down would control the money supply, and inflation, better than interest rate changes do, but that this would be politically unpalatable to rich people. Nevertheless, excess public money has to be retrieved from where it goes, and money always ends up with the rich people (regardless of how it gets to them); therefore, TAX THE VERY RICH!

The rich, by definition, are those who gain much more money than they could ever need or genuinely earn. But don't get sucked in by the conservative trope: 'Oh look, it's the politics of envy!' People trapped in poverty are not 'envious' of the extravagantly rich – no, they are more likely *enraged* by the injustice of the system that privileges the few and trashes the many. Our government only needs to tax the mega-rich just enough to curb their performative extravagance, their displays of conspicuous consumption. If progressive income tax rates are varied around the point where excess demand and over-consumption are curbed (e.g. 'statement' cars and high-fashion should be taxed heavily), then that would be a beneficial policy. Appropriately high income and asset taxes on the uber-rich would suppress demand-pull inflation harmlessly while having a positive effect on the problem of over-consumption. This would be much better than the current goods and services tax, which every consumer must pay and which every business must collect. Apart from being much more efficient, taxes on the rich are fairer because the GST hurts the poor proportionately harder than the rich. That's to say, any GST is regressive.

One estimate I've heard is that the RBA creates only about 20% of our money. Some comes from government spending, but most of our supply of new money (numbers) comes from the commercial banks as described above. I submit that it's the private banks that really influence the money supply, and that easy credit and household debt are among the biggest drivers of inflation. Curiously, then RBA Governor, Philip Lowe, thought the RBA was the *only* body able to create money in Australia. To illustrate this, here's a snippet of a response by Governor Lowe to then Senator Rex Patrick at a Senate Select Committee hearing:

> **Philip Lowe**: *The source of the Reserve Bank's money – this is the beauty of central banking: central banks are unique entities in that they can create money. When we want to buy a government bond from a pension fund, the way we pay for that is credit – if*

you buy it from a bank – at the bank's account at the Reserve Bank. We are the one entity in the country that can create money just out of nothing. That's why it's incredibly important that the governance around that process is very strong, and that, as I said in response to Senator Whish-Wilson's question, is why the separation of monetary and fiscal policy is kept.

(Here he means that he has to keep politicians away from his blank cheque-book (*our* money tree) because pollies can't be trusted – whether their intentions are cynical or social. Apparently, the establishment members of the RBA Board are the only ones wise enough to dispense the fruits of Australia's money tree. (So *why* did the RBA invest billions of dollars in Government bonds and keep interest rates near zero under the L/NP regime, yet stopped buying bonds when the ALP looked like winning the 2022 election and jacked up interest rates as fast as they could get away with?)

Philip Lowe continued: *We have seen, where that has not been maintained, that it can be abused – creating money out of thin air and financing government expenditure without checks and balances.*

Rex Patrick commented: *It sounds like a great job, if you don't mind me saying!*

Philip Lowe continued: *The governance of it is incredibly important. It's mainly about interest rates, but the central banks are the only entities that can create money out of thin air. We take that responsibility incredibly seriously, and it's not to be abused.*

Abusing it is what the RBA *has* been doing, I submit.

No matter who is creating (and destroying?) Australia's currency, evidently our federal government and all currency-issuing governments have the power to pay for whatever the country truly *needs* and therefore they should do exactly that. Added to which, it's obvious that our government owned bank, the people's bank, i.e. the RBA, must be made transparent, accountable, democratic, more egalitarian, and much more responsible to the parliament – rather than being controlled by the secretive, overpaid academics and rich, establishment business-people, who meet with financiers, bosses, and other corporate-captured folk in order to manipulate whatever they can in the service of money instead of in the service of the people of Australia. It doesn't have to be this way. To fix all this, the people must demand that our government radically restructure the machinery of the current system, and reform it for the provision of a fair, healthy, and happy Australian society. (I'd like to see the RBA abolished and its functions absorbed into, and performed better, by a re-nationalised Commonwealth Bank, as per the 1945 Banking Act.)

As stated above, the core of MMT is the truth that a currency-issuing government does not have a budget like a household budget where the **income-over-outgo ratio** (I call it 'Micawber's ratio' – see Dickens's *David Copperfield*) has to be always greater than 1 (one), otherwise it is sinking into poverty. A currency-issuing government does not need to maintain a budget surplus but instead can simply write a cheque in order to spend where spending is needed. The Australian Government doesn't need to 'borrow to build'; it writes the cheques and cashes them. That was the key Franklin Roosevelt used to unlock economic activity to end the Great Depression of the 1930s – so, not such a modern theory. (However FDR was another 'kitchen-budget literalist' regarding money, and was reluctant to continue deficit spending.) The only limit to the power of deficit spending is the underlying capacity of the economy itself. That can be hard to estimate. There is always plenty of work to be done; it just needs someone (a government) to pay for it if the privateers can't (or shouldn't) get a profit from it. Plus, there is always a lot of work done that is not paid for, or measured, in a national economy – all the unpaid work done mostly by women to start with. So, it's a myth that it's a bad thing for governments to run a deficit. A federal deficit may only mean the government wrote more in cheques than it got back in tax.

The other accounting stream is when the government sells debt notes (IOUs such as bonds etc), it effectively borrows from the private sector to increase the numbers in its accounts, but our public money has to pay the interest on those 'borrowings' until the RBA buys back the debt notes and cancels them. Again, a government that issues its own fiat currency ***does not*** need to issue debt. The main reason it does so is to please the Foreign Exchange money traders (so they bid it higher than other currencies) and to open that conduit for public money to go to the financial institutions. I must repeat that. The ***only*** reason a currency issuing government issues debt is to channel public money to banks, finance houses and other rich people, and so that the money marketeers all stay happy.

A corollary to the power of federal money is that we don't need **Foreign Investment**. This may surprise some folks and be disputed by many, but think on it. If a profitable project needs money to start it, then the federal government can write all the cheques and reap the rewards when the project is profitable. Of course the government would have to be careful that they didn't over-extend economic capacity, waste public money or detrimentally divert resources from where they were needed more. But conversely, if a foreign company comes to your country and starts a project, when the project turns a profit the foreign company is going to want all its investment back, plus a handsome profit. There are not many reasons for a foreigner to invest in your country unless it's to take away a profit. Few investors are altruists. So all foreign investment ends in a net loss of wealth to your country. Worst case scenario is if the foreign company isn't even taxed reasonably. This has sometimes suited countries because they gauge that the net loss of wealth may have an offset that they desire, such as employing a lot of people. But the myth that foreign money is needed has left a lot of resource-rich countries sitting in poverty while the big companies exploit them and expatriate the wealth. The myth of foreign investment has also led to a sort of Cargo Cult mentality in many places. That's true of my state, Tasmania, where many of the islanders are always looking for the next 'Big Thing'. The policy of Hydro-industrialisation was to develop the state's hydro electric potential and lure big foreign companies to set up power-hungry industries in order to employ the locals. That's been very profitable for all the companies that took up the offer. At the Risdon Zinc works, where I worked for a short time, it was said that the profit just from the Sulphuric acid plant was enough to pay all the wages of the factory, everything else was profit taken overseas.

Another corollary of the power of a sovereign currency is that there shouldn't be any need to borrow money from overseas lenders such as the **International Monetary Fund** (IMF). This institution was set up with good intentions in 1945 as one of the outcomes of the 1944 Bretton Woods Conference. It's a long story, but the IMF has since become dominated by neoliberal economics, and instead of being a benevolent lender of last resort it has used the leverage of its loans to impose neoliberal conditions on many countries – measures such as domestic austerity, open trade, free capital movements, and foreign ownership – measures which tended to favour American companies.

Based in Washington, the IMF has essentially been using **debt traps** to serve US financial interests. But here's the kicker, if a country controls its fiat currency carefully the sovereign government can do all the internal investing it needs and can marshal all its human capital in the service of its own people. If a nation doesn't have an independent currency then it should want to create one. The problem with this comes when that nation wants to trade with others and its currency's exchange rate is at junk status on the Forex money markets. It's this free-market in money that has given the $USD so much leverage and which tends to keep the poor countries poor, despite often being resource rich. The solution to this cruel purchasing power imbalance is, as I explain elsewhere, to peg your national fiat currency to an immutable measure of value (e.g. an hour of labour) and to build international trade relationships which thereby ensure fair **purchasing power parity** (PPP).

FISCAL INEQUITY BETWEEN THE TIERS OF GOVERNMENT

The difference between a currency-issuing national government and the other tiers of government is stark. State and Territory governments have to rely on grants from the federal government and whatever small taxes and fees they can charge themselves. The third tier of government, our municipal or shire councils, have a relatively secure revenue base in the property tax we call 'rates'. But I must emphasize the enormous difference in power this gives to a currency issuing government, especially compared to the states which are currency consuming governments. This means that the states and territories are largely mendicant to Australia's federal government. Apart from that, they have to rely on some fair taxes like mining royalties, dividends from government owned businesses, or else some unfair and regressive taxes like stamp duty (a conveyance levy), plus fines, fees, and a state land tax – which is imposed on *top of* the land / property tax that the third tier of government is already levying, namely, municipal rates. Otherwise, state governments might issue debt that (sadly) they must pay back and pay interest on.

At the time of writing it's said that Tasmania has a debt of $3.5 billion, which is forecast to grow to $8.5 billion in four years time. For a small state with dubious income that is really quite bad. The state has a large unfunded superannuation liability and has to pay interest on its present debt, yet it's not doing very well at providing the services of health and education that we ought to be able to expect at this time. The present government wants to build a billion dollar football stadium and has other infrastructure plans while not saying a word about climate change. In the same week that the 2024 state budget was brought down, some powerful winds and stormy weather had wrecked substantial areas of the power grid and left thousands without electricity for many days. The harmful effects of climate change are just starting, but neither Tasmania nor any other Australian government is taking it seriously.

Using Tasmania as an example, the bulk of the state's revenue comes from federal allocations, purportedly from the GST. This is collected by the federal government and distributed among the states, but maybe it just comes out of consolidated revenue – whatever that is. Payments from the federal government, including from the GST pool and commonwealth specific purpose payments (SPPs), make up 65% of income for the Tasmanian government. Other revenue comes from various sources such as a stamp duty that's a disincentive to moving house, a state-based land tax which is doubled onto the property tax called municipal rates, some mining royalties that are probably too lenient, payroll tax which penalises employers for employing anyone, plus some revenue comes from fees, and licences which nobody likes. This is obviously a somewhat scrappy tax base, and although Tasmania gets a reasonable share of the national GST, the aggregate is still not enough to provide public health and education properly. This must change.

To belabour the point about federal-state fiscal inequity, here's a quote from Wikipedia on Income Tax in Australia.

> *The first income tax in Australia was imposed in 1884 by South Australia with a general tax on income. Federal income tax was first introduced in 1915, as a wartime measure to help fund Australia's war effort in the First World War. Between 1915 and 1942, income taxes were levied by both State governments and the federal government. In 1942, to help fund World War II, the federal government took over the raising of all income tax, to the exclusion of the States. The loss of the states' ability to raise revenue via income tax was offset by federal government grants to the states.*

And for those who think today's top marginal tax rate is too high:

> *In 1951, the top marginal tax rate for incomes above £10,000* [equivalent to $425,000 today] *was 75%. And from 1955 until the mid-1980s the top marginal tax rate was 67%.*

Given that the states gave up all their best sources of revenue for the federal government to fight wars, it seems overdue for the federal government to either give back the taxation powers or else take over the major tasks that the state governments are struggling to fulfill. Most obviously would be the public hospitals and public health, plus the underfunded public schools. The federal government has all the resources needed to end ambulance ramping and improve child literacy (for example), so the feds should use our public money to actually provide all the major public services.

While we're dreaming, if the federal government scrapped AUKUS, cancelled the useless tanks and long-range missiles (using diplomacy instead of military spending to maintain peace), then they could cancel all HECS debts and fund TAFE and University education 100% free, as the Whitlam government did. With regard to national security (and much else) it's astonishing how governments tend to confront software problems with hardware solutions. This is analogous to threatening your computer with a hammer when one of its programs plays up. If Australians wants peace in our region we should be talking to our neighbours, not threatening them with wars we certainly wouldn't win. The reader will guess that I support the Independent and Peaceful Australia Network (IPAN).

Returning to fiscal inequity, we should always use the correct terms. It is 'rate-payer's money' (land/property tax-payer's money) in local/municipal government. At the state level it is 'public money' (from federal grants) and 'fee-payer's money' (from state fees). At the federal level it is always 'public money' because the federal government is not tax-dependent. This is important because politicians are keen to use the term 'taxpayers' money' as if the federal government depended on tax, which it doesn't. And the misnomer suggests it's only people who are rich enough to pay tax who keep the government in funds, and also that it's the quantum of revenue that limits what our federal government can afford. Both those popular misconceptions are so false that anyone who uses the term 'taxpayers' money' is perpetuating a lie, a cruel deceit. Federal money is public money!

DEBT

Raising debt always means a net loss to the borrower, and that includes our people's government. Currency-issuing governments do not need to raise debt in their own currency. The only reason they do this is to provide interest-bearing assets to rich people, banks, and finance houses. This is an example of what Professor Yanis Varoufakis, in his 2023 book, *Techno Feudalism: What Killed Capitalism*, calls **socialism for the bankers**. The debt instruments are essentially a conduit for public money to go to the wealthy top-end of the private sector. Selling bonds etc to this sector means the government's accounts go into deficit and the so-called *National Debt* – resulting from all the needlessly issued debt instruments – balloons out cheerfully. The public sector's national debt is the private sector's asset and income-stream. A non-capitalist might suggest that the public's money would be of more use channeled through health, education, and a thousand other community needs, rather than through the rich sector that does not need it. But dedicated capitalists would say actions like solving the problems of the health sector, lifting welfare so people could buy food and medicine (and didn't have to turn to crime), and making education egalitarian and free, would be a waste of money.

In that part of his book Yanis Varoufakis was describing events during the 2008 Global Financial Crisis (GFC) in which governments 'printed' large amounts of money to bail out the failing banks, then let the culpable bankers go unpunished with big salaries, yet imposed harsh austerity on the working class. Governments found the money for the financiers (socialism for the banks), but the people who had lost their houses, superannuation or savings and many had to work harder for longer to recover their losses. A proposition in *Techno Feudalism* is that with the rise of the mega-corporations of the Internet, such as Amazon and Google, the West is moving away from profit-based capitalism into a rent-based neo-feudalism where the big media and trade corporations (e.g. Meta & Amazon) are the new feudal overlords, and we the people are their compliant vassals and serfs.

Another good reason why spending by a currency-issuing government should be restricted to real needs (rather than overpaid consultants and the phallic fantasies of the militarists such as submarines and missiles) is that too much money can find its way to rich people whose desires-plus-disposable-cash can tempt price-setters to push up prices; i.e. cause inflation.

While rich people are able to park a lot of money in tax-avoiding bank accounts and yacht basins, the rising cost-of-living (*aka* inflation) hurts all those workers who can't increase their own incomes. Also, if the government fails to get the public's money back from the rich sector (through tax), then the money supply can grow to inflationary levels. The L/NP federal regime ran Australia's national debt to over a million millions of dollars (so-called 'trillion') with its deficit spending during the Covid Pandemic, and they didn't care about it because the RBA bought lots of debt notes and the finance houses grew rich. Yet the Coalition were quite mean about paying for essential public services like health, education, child and aged care, social security, the arts, universities, and other vital services – which they excused in the name of 'fiscal austerity', but which was really just because the L/NP and the ALP-Right have little sympathy for jobseekers, the aged, students, academics, or anyone who's poor. It is classist and racist, but neoliberalism has its 'teacher's pets' too, namely, the excessively rich. 'Socialism for the rich' is the true character of neoliberal economics. (Thanks for the term, Robert Reich.)

The Right-wing are quick to criticise **government spending** when they're in opposition, but they very happily move billions of dollars of public money to the private sector when in government. That doesn't stop them punching-down in a classist way. Applying socialism for the banks (and military), austerity for the poor and generosity to the rich is the L/NP's chief purpose. We only need to mention the deadly 'Robodebt' scam again to indicate the depths to which their cruel stupidity sank. No austerity is needed by a sensible sovereign government.

And those who say government spending (on essential services and/or social support) is inflationary are either fools or liars. Even veteran economist Chris Richardson claimed in January 2024 to the effect that if the government gave cost of living relief to poor people it would fuel inflation. This is nonsense because he should know that the price-setters set prices at the point where rich people are prepared to pay, and they ignore the poor people because the poor can't pay anyway. Government spending, on things like roads, housing or welfare, doesn't go directly to the rich so it is not a temptation to price-setters. But higher interest and tax cuts *do* feed money to the rich; whose demand *does* tempt price-setters.

Inflation is not so much about the quantity of money in the economy, but rather it's about *who* has that money and what they're doing with it. As TIA chief economist Richard Denniss wrote on 19th of May 2023:

> *It is not true that increasing government spending will make inflation worse. It's also no accident that those opposed to small increases in unemployment benefits – arguing it will cause inflation and worsen the cost of living – have been strategically silent about the impact of spending $268–368 billion on the AUKUS submarines* [or the original Stage 3 Tax Cuts]. *Does anyone really believe that spending money on the poor will harm us and spending money on the rich will help us? Welcome to the topsy-turvy world of Australian economic debate.*

Most of Australia's recent inflation has been caused by profiteering price-setters chasing the excess money of rich people. Services, rents and goods are all priced for the wealthy. Prices are set at the maximum level just below where buyers start refusing to pay, but those buyers include the rich folk who can afford high prices. Prices are rarely set fairly for the low income earners to afford – maybe only in tip-shops and op-shops.

In truth, **monetarists who deploy the higher interest-rates lever are punishing mortgagees for the inflation caused by price-gouging corporations** – like our supermarket duopoly.

High wealth occurs because some people have unfairly high incomes. Incomes have lost all contact with reality when the CEOs of banks or airlines are sent home with annual incomes in the region of $25 million or more. It is this unjust inequality and low taxes on the rich that are the true drivers of inflation. The federal government can fix this by taxing the rich much more with properly progressive taxes and by legally requiring price-setters and high wage earners to publicly justify their pursuit of ever more money.

If he were alive today, Australia's first post-WWII prime minister, the great Ben Chifley would hate what's happening to the RBA. As an architect of the charter of our present RBA, Chifley would be saddened that the Labor-initiated review of 2022 has only served to erode the responsibilities of the RBA and to entrench monetarism even further. He would hate that the RBA is being run by academic-monetarists and ultra-capitalists only for the enrichment of capitalists, and he'd hate how Treasurer Chalmers was encouraged to give away his veto of RBA decisions, and therefore all leverage over the RBA. Fortunately, in mid 2024 Dr Chalmers was persuaded to keep the veto, albeit to use it as a last resort.

It was said Ben Chifley joked that he was cursed with the ability to understand economics, so he'd hate the extent to which the RBA has abandoned its charter, and he would be enraged that the RBA has been abusing the working people of Australia so badly, for so long, and is still getting away with it. Chifley would be sad the Labor Party has lost its 'light-on-the-hill' vision and has become a centre-right party, captured by corporations and serving the profiteering of big-business rather than maintaining the fair and egalitarian democracy most Australians hoped to enjoy. As the Prime Minister who correctly tried to control inflation by controlling price-gouging from Canberra, and as the PM who, with remarkable prescience, wanted to nationalise the private banks, Chifley would be deeply angry at the way Australia is now so unfair and unequal, betrayed by neoliberalism and the Tories, and he would be aggrieved by the ALP's part in that betrayal. I think Chifley would be appalled by the way in which the ALP government is complying with neoliberal economic dogma.

Neoliberal free-market ideology has demanded lower government controls on banks. The Australian financial sector is all but fully deregulated in line with neoliberal economic policy. Milton Friedman's monetarism has been Australia's economic orthodoxy since 1983. Sadly, the review into the RBA that was conducted by the Labor government in 2022 has improved nothing – if anything it has made matters worse. We could hardly expect it to improve the RBA because the review was conducted by monetarists. Now the RBA board will meet less often, has had a little rearranging, and has a new governor, Michele Bullock, but otherwise it will stay on exactly the same course. However, as stated above, the RBA will abandon its Charter obligation to address 'The economic prosperity and welfare of the people of Australia'. We 'missed a bullet' when Treasurer Chalmers decided against forsaking his last-resort power to veto RBA decisions. Although that power is little used, its abolition would have given far too much power and autonomy to the unelected and unaccountable RBA cabal of group-thinking monetarists. For the government to give away control of monetary policy to such a body, for the purpose of being able to blame harmful policy on someone else, would have been outrageous. As WWII PM John Curtin said:

If the Government of the Commonwealth deliberately excluded itself from all participation in the making or changing of monetary policy it cannot govern except in a secondary degree.

As I write, Greens' Senator Nick McKim is trying to get ALP Treasurer Chalmers to force the RBA to reduce the interest rates, but Governor Bullock wants to keep punishing borrowers. Nick is right, of course, if the government was doing enough, you know, actual governing, then the RBA should never have raised the rates in the first place. More explanation will follow.

There is nothing morally or practically superior about having a publicly funded and owned 'independent' body (the RBA) supposedly trying to control price-gouging corporations by raising interest rates – rather than a publicly funded authority, answerable to our elected government, that justifies all prices and salaries. Rather, one could argue the opposite. Also, given that the RBA long ago effectively abandoned its charter obligation to full employment (excusing deliberate unemployment with the mythical NAIRU), plus that it has provably failed to maintain 'the stability of the currency of Australia', one has to ask *who* the RBA is really serving. The tasks of financial management plus monetary and fiscal policy are important, but the present system is a bad joke. I genuinely think we must abolish the present RBA and restart with a new, publicly-owned, government-controlled bank that truly enacts the original charter of the RBA and actually serves the people of Australia.

INTEREST RATES

Interest rates don't need to rise because they do not have a direct influence on the choices made by the price-setters in the economy. Rather, it is indirect reactions like anti-gouging protests, Senate enquiries, and the ACTU-commissioned inquiry into price-gouging that induce price-setters to slow their profiteering, which is why economists see a so-called 'lag' of about a year between interest hikes and moderating price rises. Higher interest rates eventually cause enough damaging wealth-shift from workers to lucky savers that inflation slows, but not in a fair way. **Interest rate rises do not slow inflation**. Rather, higher interest channels money to the rich, whose 'demand' pulls up prices. So, exactly opposite to the stated aim of increased interest rates, this action tends to **cause more** inflation, even as it gouges borrowers. And to emphasise this point, in June 2024 RBA governor Bullock, Treasurer Chalmers, and a number of commentators echoed each other, saying that inflation is '*sticky*'. Such a technical term! In other words, they don't have a clue!

There are four main things that influence price rises: supply, demand, expectation, and greed. Firstly there are fluctuations in the availability or cost of supplies (called 'cost-push' inflation). Secondly there's demand by buyers with money to spend (called 'demand-pull' inflation). While there have been some cost-push on prices in Australia, it's been deceptive of authorities to blame our inflation on foreign wars. (Also, the RBA hasn't explained how interest rate rises could slow cost-push inflation, because of course, they cannot!) Thirdly there's what's called 'built-in inflation', which is where people expect current inflation rates to continue. This 'inflation of expectation' is what the RBA relies upon to have us accept its so-called target annual inflation of 2–3%, which is really only for the benefit of businesses selling goods and services. People talk about a 'wage-price spiral' that doesn't exist in practice because wage rises almost never occur before price rises – rises always lead. Along with the steady loss of purchasing power, workers are always disadvantaged by inflation. As for the fourth cause of unjustified price rises, one only needs to note the unexplained leap in the prices of everything in the supermarkets in order to 'smell a rat', and millions of Australians have done just that. One big rat is the supermarket duopoly.

This fourth and biggest cause of inflation should be called Price-Gouge inflation, or as someone dubbed it, 'greedflation'. It's driven by price-setters. As outlined above, advertising works on consumers to cause 'demand-pull' price rises. Buyers with too much money chasing too few goods are tempting the price-setters to raise prices excessively and gouge their customers. But demand-pull inflation is always blamed on greedy buyers while letting the greedy price-setters off the hook. Price-gouging is simply raising prices far above a justified cost plus a fair profit. One trick the supermarkets pull is putting their prices up and down to confuse customers. The ACCC is pursuing the supermarket duopoly for deceptively dropping their boosted prices and calling them 'specials' when they really aren't. The profit mark-up on goods might be a modest 10% sometimes, though usually much higher, but sometimes the profit margin might be 300% or more! Unfair profit amounts to theft. Theft is immoral; hence the pejorative term 'price-gouge'. No matter how factors combine to raise prices, Price-Gouge inflation is a real phenomenon and should be much more condemned by economists and politicians. It is now mandatory to display the cost per unit of measure in supermarkets, the so-called unit-price, but it should also be mandatory for sellers to display their degree of profiteering on all goods and services by displaying the mark-up clearly. When consumers are armed with more knowledge about how prices are set, then they are empowered to obtain a fairer transaction. Such knowledge would also put brakes on the arcane process of determining the consumer price index which in turn (along with employment numbers and other measures) helps to inform the RBA in their decisions whether to raise or lower interest rates.

Interest-rates on mortgages are not counted in the consumer price index (CPI). This obscures the inflationary effect of mortgage increases, so the RBA gets much less blame for *creating* inflation than they deserve. But interest rates should be counted along with rising rents because mortgage repayments are in the column marked 'out-go' for millions of people. All price rises that consumers have to accept should be counted on the CPI. Every price-rise adds to the downward spiral of the purchasing power of wages and/or savings (if you have any). Every price rise, including the cost of money, should be counted as inflation.

What the RBA and every Australian government must grasp is that ***increasing interest rates actually increases inflation*** more than not.

This is not only because businesses operating on borrowed money or over-draughts have to pass on the extra cost of their borrowings, but also because higher interest on deposits sends more money to wealthy savers (by definition, if you can save you're wealthy) who are the same rich spenders who create demand-pull inflation. Interest rate rises feed more money to the banks and therefore to the bank's shareholders who are also the wealthy spenders who can chase up rising prices. At the time of writing, the last interest rates rise was on 7th of November 2023. Up till then the RBA had increased interest rates thirteen times since the L/NP lost power in the May 2022 election. The Labor government struggles to justify these rises, and both the minimum wage and government spending are blamed by the Lying/Nasty Party for the unemployment and worsening inequality that the rate rises are deliberately causing. Yet it's all a needless, useless cruelty by the RBA.

As said above, raising interest rates is a counter-productive way to curb inflation. In an essay for *The Saturday Paper* on 21st April 2023 Richard Denniss of the Australia Institute put it this way:

> *Thanks to the decisions of the current RBA board, a young couple with a mortgage of $600,000 will this year spend an extra $16,400 on repayments. ... According to the RBA, the best way to control inflation is to make millions of people spend hundreds of dollars a week extra on their loan repayments. The logic is that if billions of dollars a week are diverted from spending on groceries, clothes etc, then the firms selling those things will have to stop lifting prices. And if shops lay-off staff because customers are buying less stuff, then that lowers consumer spending as well. In formal economic language, that brutal calculus is known as 'the monetary policy transmission mechanism'.*

Again, as said earlier, raising interest rates does little more than further open the flood gates on the rivers of money flowing to the private banks, yet about 500,000 home-buying families are going backwards financially due to the sharpest rise in Australia's interest rate history. The only responsible and kind thing for the RBA to do would be to reduce the interest rates down to near zero again, steadily, but at least as fast as they cruelly (or was it maliciously?) jacked them up after the ALP won the 2022 federal election.

The ways people have disposable money are through credit, savings, or surplus income. An increased cost of money (interest rises) may deter a few from maximising their credit card debt or borrowing for consumption (like buying an unneeded new car), but for those who are struggling it simply robs from the poorer to give to the richer: reverse Robin Hood. And the richest are the majority foreign-owned banks. It's high-waged and previously-privileged people who, with high savings, can afford to be big spenders, despite higher prices. So in truth it is the *quantity* of money held by the rich, rather than the *price* of money for borrowers, which has the greater inflationary effect.

Ever since trading began there would have been a quantity of 'money' in circulation that generally reflected how much was needed to facilitate economic activity in society. That's essentially the job-description of a currency, but when great economic injustice (*aka* inequality) is allowed to grow, and the rich are swimming in it while the poor go cold and hungry, then the quantity of money *in circulation* (i.e. the money supply plus the velocity of money) is much more important. RBA bosses have boasted that (according to bank data) Australians had lots of savings, despite the Pandemic. Nonsense! They take a reading of everyone's bank savings, find the average and then pretend the number actually means something in this radically unequal society. Successive governors of the RBA have conveniently ignored the high numbers of people who are living from payday to payday with zero savings in their accounts. Soon after being appointed as the new governor Michele Bullock told a meeting that Australians were financially okay. If the RBA sees only those who have money saved (i.e. those who are rich), then they'll blithely keep putting up interest rates. And this delusion of general wealth will encourage price-setters to keep putting up prices – at least until a lot of people start screaming, STOP!

Once again, this can be fixed – not by giving tax cuts to the rich but by seriously increasing the progressive taxes *on* the rich. In the 1960s governments did 'control the money supply' by changing tax rates. Since neoliberalism polluted the common mind, no politician would be brave enough to do it again, yet it would tend to discourage the idiotically high incomes of CEOs *et al*, even though it may not be enough. All corporations should be forced to pay reasonable tax on net-profits, and all governments need to be able to claw back more than the internationally agreed 15% from tax-haven accounts. Sadly, this may be difficult because so many of our politicians also suffer from corporate-capture.

What's meant by **corporate-capture** is when a corporation captures the mind and efforts of one or many individuals. In a way it's the psychological inclination of us human animals to keep returning to our most convenient food source – in other words, to 'know which side our bread is buttered'. Or else it's caving-in to the old adage 'who pays the piper, calls the tune'. This manifests as unthinking and unquestioning obedience to those 'authorities' or employers who are feeding money and perks to the all-too-willing enabler of their doctrines and dictates. Corporate capture is manifest in people's subservience to a corporation, especially where that corporation is so big that the unthinking enabler is fully immersed in its group-think and cannot see any validity in another point of view.

Examples include the following: soldiers who blindly follow orders; academics who follow whatever orthodoxy their lecturers are teaching (e.g. today's Neoliberal economic dogma); bureaucrats who follow the political zeitgeist; media commentators who follow the corporate line (e.g. News Corp 'hosts' mindlessly obeying Murdoch's anti-science climate denial); and politicians who obey the wishes of the fossil-fuel lobby because they get paid (one way or another) as a result.

Obviously, corporate-capture corrupts our democracy and turns many people into the willing enablers of more corrupt, cunning, cruel, and even violent 'leaders'. The reason that corporate-capture is such a threat to our well-being and ultimate survival is because it facilitates misinformation, perpetuates lies, inhibits our adaptability, and we can so easily become one of its victims. If we are going to power-down/contract to a sustainable economic system, ensure sustainable agriculture, enable egalitarian democracy, slow global heating, and restore the health of the biosphere of Spaceship Earth, then we will all need to be devotees of science and truth and be hyper-vigilant in resisting corporate-capture.

Apart from its maladaptive potential, another danger in corporate-capture is that it is the same unthinking compliance that enables dictatorships of every variety. When a whole government gets taken in by one or more corporations, it's called **State Capture**. (Examples include Tasmania beholden to foreign-owned fish-farming and the AFL corporations, or Australia allowing American military corporations to dictate our foreign policy.) Lobbyists are paid by corporations to stalk our politicians and convince them to act for the good of the owners of capital rather than for the good of the people. You know there's capture when criticism and dissent are suppressed and voices of reason ridiculed.

FASCISM

It is unquestioning group-think and corporate-capture which, to a lesser or greater degree, forms part of the syndrome called fascism. I highlight this because knowing what mind-set to avoid in daily life, and ensuring it doesn't get elected to power, may be as important as any other element of political awareness. The term fascist has often been used as a random term of abuse, but I think it's important that voters are fully aware of the syndrome in order to be able to recognise and resist it. Fascism may begin as a malaise of crony-corruption that spreads too easily in society. The best people resist it, but it is insidious. Wikipedia describes it like this:

> **Fascism** *is a far-right, authoritarian, ultranationalist political ideology and movement, characterized by a dictatorial leader,*

centralised autocracy, militarism, forcible suppression of opposition, belief in a natural social hierarchy, subordination of individual interests for the perceived good of the nation or race and strong regimentation of society and the economy. Opposed to anarchism, democracy, pluralism, liberalism, socialism, and Marxism, fascism is placed on the far-right wing within the traditional left-right spectrum.

I would say that fascism is a money-idolizing, psychological syndrome that grips males more often than females, but it's not exclusively a male project. Women can be enablers of a dictatorial leader or dictatorship (e.g. a military junta) nearly as much as men, but misogyny and toxic masculinity are certainly part of fascism. A major goal of fascists is to achieve political power for its own sake. Fascism includes shameless corruption, contempt for human rights, the arts, education, intellectuals, science, and for females. Fascists prefer totalitarian nation-state control and a hierarchical-patriarchy. They glorify violence, and as their in-group unifier they enjoy hating minorities and out-groups. Fascists are intolerant of difference and like to persecute minorities. A fascist regime will suppress all opposition and ignore or crush dissent. Fascists hate diversity, pluralism, democracy, and/or the rule of law. Fascists are pack-predators, they are aggressively racist, ultra-nationalist, militarist and uniform-loving conformists. Fascists tend to be classist, misogynist, group-thinking, anti-liberal, corporate-captured, religionists and crony-capitalists. Obviously, this male dominated, self-serving, ethos-of-domination is disastrous if it infects your community – or worse, if it gains political power. In October 2024, before the US presidential elections, retired General Mark Milley warned that Donald Trump is 'fascist to the core' and called Trump *the most dangerous person in this country* [the US]. As 'First Dog on the Moon' cartoonist for Guardian Australia wrote, 'I suspect it's not a good thing when you are too fascist for the US Army.' A telling quote from Gustave Gilbert, a US Army psychologist assigned to work with the Nazi defendants at the Nuremberg trials, is this: *Evil, I think, is the absence of empathy.*

There is a strong case that Australia's L/NP regime (2013–2022) sank into this fascist pattern or syndrome. To a regrettable extent, they took the federal public service with them. Starting with greedy, venal, self-serving, crony-capitalism, a culture of careless, classist corruption seeped into everything the L/NP touched. That regime appointed so many of their cronies to positions of power and influence that it will take many years before integrity and a non-partisan culture fully returns to the commonwealth public service. Unfortunately, over recent decades there has been a determined effort to push Australians' political mind-set towards the Right and have us all accept this fascist-leaning neoliberalism.

Unfortunately too there have been a significant number of bully-boy neo-fascists elected to power around the globe in recent times. I won't name them for fear of a death squad visiting, but you can guess who they are. Those quasi-dictators who have death squads murdering their dissenters are ... well, by their fruits you will know them. Matthew 7:16–20.

A mind-set of far-right, climate-science-dismissing, neo-fascist nastiness has been steadily pushed and promoted by the Murdoch (News Corp) propaganda juggernaut. I wouldn't want to be gulled by paranoid conspiracy theories, but a look at the history of the Atlas Network, its affiliates and supporters, makes it evident that all would-be democracies are up against a global right-wing conspiracy. The Murdochs and News Corp have been in the thick of this, and the News Corp lackeys are still poisoning the minds of a large number of Australians to this day. Here are some references and reading.

First there's Dr Jeremy Walker's article on The Atlas Network:

> https://epress.lib.uts.edu.au/journals/index.php/mcs/article/view/8813

Then there's the 2024 book *The Invisible Doctrine: The Secret History of Neoliberalism (& How It Came To Control Your Life)* by Peter Hutchison and George Monbiot.

And also, 'Led by Donkeys' on the Murdoch political evil:

> https://www.youtube.com/watch?v=_ZcYu0NOpuM

The crimes that the Murdoch juggernaut has committed should eventually be tried in The Hague. Not their only but their worst crime has been their endless abuse against climate science (lying, really), which has contributed to the world missing our best chance at slowing the global heating that will eventually kill billions of innocent people.

There is a deep set of connections and a mutually supportive relationship between the fossil-fuel-backed Atlas Network, the far-Right 'think tanks' like Australia's IPA, Pentagon-backed ASPI, Murdoch's News Corp, and the far-Right members of the L/NP coalition. The past L/NP regime seemed to relish projects for punching-down on the less privileged. From the cruelty of jailing refugees in remote prisons, for up to 10 years, to the lethal, immoral and illegal Robodebt scam, the L/NP bully-managed everyone from first nations people to the women in their own team. They disdained good governance and deliberately sabotaged any action to slow global heating. The L/NP coalition cannot be believed about anything because they only care about themselves and their mates. The federal L/NP, especially under Dutton, have made themselves enemies of the people.

The syndrome can be tricky to identify. People are afflicted by this ruthless lust for power and money to greater or lesser degrees. The capitalist cultural mindset teaches us to crave money and promotion, so the seeds of greed and the lust for power are already sown. The syndrome affects people differently and also changes over time. It can range from favours-for-the-mates corruption through to the fully heartless, murdering Nazi. The degree to which we are prepared to lie and cheat and hurt others for money and power indicates how much the fascist syndrome has infected us. Decent people try not to go so low, and most people are not fascist at all. It can be hard to tell how toxic a person is from how they look or what they say, but they reveal themselves by what they do. In his 2011 book entitled *The Psychopath Test*, Jon Ronson expands on the work of the Canadian psychologist, Professor Robert D. Hare. Ronson points out that our era has seen a lot of men appointed to top positions who display high degrees of this anti-social personality disorder. Since a lying, cheating fraud has been re-elected POTUS, we will soon learn how dangerous he is. What Australia does *not* need is such a character to become Prime Minister.

While we're discussing whom to be wary of, **beware the demagogues**. A demagogue is defined in Wikipedia as:

> *... a person who pursues power by pandering to or exciting the popular passions and prejudices of their audience; one who attempts to control the multitude by specious or deceitful* [lying] *arts, or by carelessly scape-goating out-groups, and exaggerating the dangers from out-groups to stoke racist/ xenophobic fears.*

Such a person is one who thinks nothing of lying for emotional effect:

> *... an unprincipled and fact-denying mob-orator or political rabble rouser.*

These are people who knowingly say things that are false, or raise a trivial diversion, in the confident knowledge that sooner or later their lies will be believed by enough people to serve their purpose. That well-known American advisor to demagogues, Steve Bannon, put it this way, 'You have to flood the zone with shit'. Our previous PM, Morrison was a habitual liar who lied even when he didn't need to – more Dumbo than demagogue. In the UK, we see vacuous loud-mouths such as Tommy Robinson, in Europe it's Marine Le Pen, and others, while in the US the most dangerous (but not the only) lying braggart is D. J. Trump. Narcissists, psychopaths and demagogues will, by default, blame economic problems on the most opportune out-group and blame such troubles as the rising cost of living on whoever they decide they want to demonise and diminish most at the time. For example, ever since being elected to parliament Ms P. Hanson has blamed Indigenous and Asian Australians for the economic effects of neoliberalism. Likewise, Mr Dutton has fear-mongered over nonthreatening African gangs, China, refugees, and others in order to garner votes among the easily-frightened electorate. At the time of writing, the L/NP is blaming inflation, high rents, and high house prices on recently arrived immigrants.

Inflation again

Australia, and many other countries, are experiencing high inflation. In 2023, price rises in Australia peaked at a rate around 7% per annum, but little of that was necessary. It caused serious cost-of-living anxiety, especially for the less well-off among us. As explained already, constantly rising prices (rising out-go) erode the purchasing power of our incomes and savings. But prices don't rise by themselves; the people tasked with raising the prices are hard at work! I call them price-setters. Price rises routinely pre-date wage rises, which gives the price-setters the constant lead over wage earners. By wage earners, I mean those who can't set their own wages, not the executives who *can* keep increasing their salaries. Wage earners almost never catch up with or get ahead of price rises. Price rises also erode our sense of what a thing is worth to us – or at least of how to judge the value of goods and services in monetary terms. It's called 'unanchored expectations'; it's partly why inflation is 'maintained' and it's another cog in the system. With this failing sense of value, the rising prices give a house-edge advantage to those sellers who can also be price-setters. The price-setters can keep raising their prices because the inflationary environment keeps the price-taking buyer wrong-footed and not knowing what's worth what. Whoever's had the slightest brush with **game theory** will recognise that this asymmetrical 'knowledge' between price-setters and price-takers always gives the price-setters the advantage. As noted above, price rises leading wage rises (inflation) gives business owners a games advantage which is why our business-preferencing governments and RBA are determined to deliberately maintain a constant level of inflation/price-rises. There would be much less capacity for unfair price adjustments if our currency was anchored to something that has a permanent and immutable value (for example, one hour of unassisted manual labour).

The other effect of price rises is that inflation causes our money to be partially failing in its job description (see later notes). The deliberate maintenance of inflation (as performed by the RBA) is a cruel deprivation of our sense of value. Due to this RBA policy, we are forced to tolerate the steady erosion of the value (purchasing power) of our income and savings. It has been a deliberate policy to try to keep inflation at a higher level than wage rises (so that the real value of our wages is reduced), and we've been conditioned to accept this. Only the robust unions have been able to fight back for wage rises to counter this anti-worker policy. Although we've been conditioned to accept constant inflation, when price rises become too rapid, as they have recently, then normal customers/workers become anxious because they know they are going backwards financially much more rapidly than usual.

Australia's high inflation has constantly been blamed on cost-push effects due to Covid and the war in Ukraine (US-NATO militarism versus Putin's nostalgia for Stalin's USSR) or Zionism versus Hamas in Gaza. But, if it was all cost-push inflation, then interest rate rises could never touch it. Raising interest rates has zero effect on rising energy prices (whether cost-push or price-gouge is the cause) because the energy market sets the price and demand from consumers really has no influence on those price-setters. The only (very indirect) way in which interest rate rises can affect price rises is by making mortgagees more broke, thus less able to spend and therefore unable to pay the higher prices demanded for goods and services. But that doesn't mean that all the rich people adding to demand-pull inflation have gone away. Instead, the extra interest paid on their savings *adds* to demand-pull inflation.

Interest rate rises don't mean any real downward pressure has been put on prices – they only mean that a subset of the population (mostly young home-buyers) have been made less financially secure and more likely to fall off the home-ownership ladder for the rest of their lives. That's a rotten social outcome! During the later part of 2023, the price of services was going up faster than anything, and the cost of some goods was falling a little. Inflation was still mostly demand-pull. Higher interest rates had zero effect on the cost of services. Lawyers, dentists, *et al* can name their own price. A clever person dubbed it 'greedflation', yet as I write the RBA has kept interest rates high and still might increase rates for a 14th time. One has to ask, how does stressing home buyers and forcing them to give more money to the banks, or forcing up rents on homes and businesses, prevent specialists or consultants from upping their hourly fees? It's nonsense!

If the mortgagees are investor-landlords, then they will likely pass on the interest rate rises to their tenants by raising rents and making their poor tenants poorer. Given that a third of Australians are renting, interest rate rises are forcing a growing river of funds from those renters to the banks via the conduit of negatively-geared investment-property loans to investor-landlords. Note, too, that millions of shops are rented from property-investors – are they gouging those businesses into bankruptcy? The increased flow of money from borrowers to the banks helps explain how the four biggest commercial banks in Australia posted a combined $16.2 billion profit for the first half of 2023 alone!

The only genuine control of inflation would be to stop treating the invisible hand of the market like a deity and take responsibility for controlling the price-gouging price-setters. Right-wing politicians and businessmen-thieves will scream 'Socialist!' as if the act of caring for the well-being of society was a bad thing and not actually the primary role of government, but perhaps (and I hope) the far-Right, including their propagandists in the billionaire-owned media (e.g. News Corp), and their disproven, neoliberal ideology, are rapidly becoming less popular and more irrelevant to the challenges we humans are now facing.

As mentioned earlier, Roosevelt's wartime Office of Price Administration (OPA) was successful at controlling inflation – that is, until the business lobby had it shut down as soon after the war's end as possible. So a *prices and wages justification authority* would do no worse than bring more balance and fairness into our commercial and industrial relations systems. We already have a very restrictive control on the wages of the lowest paid workers, who have to fight for every cent extra while the higher paid and executives can, and do, appoint themselves huge wage increases with zero justification. We not only need to be showing the 'worth-to-society' for all wage cases (especially high salary earners), but we also need to force price-setters to show reasonable justification for all goods and service prices. I propose that our ACCC and Fair Work Commission be amalgamated and tasked with arbitrating on every price and salary in the country. That may be nearly impossible in that monitoring every price and salary would be a huge task, but I believe it would be at least worth trying to do. If, for instance, a supermarket had to apply for permission (from an independent human, not an AI) to put up any price, then that would slow inflation all by itself. The mere existence of an authority with complete oversight, where prices and salary changes had to be justified, would make everything fairer, stop inflation almost totally, and probably lower the cost of living (by ending profiteering) all at once.

COST OF LIVING

This is the biggest source of anxiety in Australia today – even though global heating probably should be that. Other countries where conservative governments have been practising neoliberal economics have also seen a 'cost of living crisis', which can be defined as a situation where the costs of everyday essentials like food, housing and energy are rising much faster than incomes. Obviously, this situation affects those on low incomes much more drastically than it affects people on high incomes. World events have been blamed for this worsening situation, and while there are some elements of truth in that (due to supply chain disruptions and the high price of gas) the brutal truth is that everything is more expensive because greed-capitalism is working very hard to maximize its take. Most of the price hikes have been choices by corporations and internal 'rent-seekers', not forced by external issues. The northern wars have not seriously affected

Australians. We should have had plenty of domestic gas since February 2022 when Russia invaded Ukraine. The price of liquid fuels has stayed much the same. Instead, it's our government's failure to legislate against price-gouging/inflation and the vicious and needless interest rate hikes that are the cause of financial suffering. Others have seen that the 'cost of living crisis' has been explained with some bogus excuses – the Juice Media called it the 'cost of corporate greed crisis'. Unfairness is a politico-economic choice, and it has a politico-economic solution. Greedflation cannot be fixed by more neoliberal greed-economics – only by politicians having the political courage to actually govern.

There may, however, be a more sinister conspiracy than the entrenched popularity of greed. When the L/NP coalition knew they were going to lose the 2022 election, they came up with the predictive slogan: "It won't be easy under Albanese". Then the RBA started putting up interest rates as fast as they could. After the election produced a Labor federal government, Peter Dutton called the Right-wing powers to rally by saying, "Our job now is to make life difficult for the Albanese Government." Next the supermarket duopoly put up their prices needlessly, landlords put up their rents, the Australian Energy Market Operator (AEMO) encouraged energy-retailer profiteering, and gas companies falsely said they were short of gas and had to drill for more. Meanwhile the Business Council of Australia did its best to minimise any increase in the minimum wage, and raising prices on goods and services (inflation) became fashionable community-wide. The rocketing cost of living hit those without secure incomes, and other negative things happened that reinforced the Right's confidence. These included the defeat of constitutional recognition of Australia's Indigenous people, the continued prosecution of whistleblowers, and the new NACC refusing to pursue the Robodebt criminals. Plus, the ALP approved dozens of new fossil fuel projects and put public money into climate-damaging projects. Then, in trying to get better legislation from the ALP the Greens Senators made the mistake of voting with the L/NP who always opposed even the most pathetic ALP ideas (like their pusillanimous housing policy) and so got dubbed 'the No-alition'. Added to all these regrettable outcomes the Murdoch media outlets continue/d their never-ending attack on Labor, the Greens, the ABC, and on the facts of climate science. So guess what, that pre-election L/NP slogan ('It won't be easy under Albanese') came true. Was that sequence of negatives all just a coincidence?

Yes, I *am* suggesting that a loose conglomerate of ill-intentioned, dishonest, greedy and self-interested individuals and institutions, orchestrated by the News Corp-L/NP nexus, have been doing their best to sabotage Australia and to hurt the people of Australia, purely in the pursuit of political power and profit. Yes, I am saying that this latest cost of living 'crisis' is mostly man-made, not needed, and more-or-less deliberate on the part of those who hate the idea of a government that might care about everyone. Things are only going to get genuinely worse in future due to the insanity of militarism, wars and global heating disasters magnifying each other, but this present cost of living issue has largely been caused by 'conservatives' who evidently don't want to conserve civilization, or life on Earth. They don't want to conserve anything except their own profits and power.

But it seems the anti-Labor gremlins are spread through the federal bureaucracy too. Earlier I mentioned the 'wrecking-crew politicians' of the L/NP, but the neoliberal fanaticism about small and impotent government extends to entrenching a wrecking-crew bureaucracy. The relatively new Urgent Care Clinics may be an example of wrecking-crew administration – a prime example of someone deliberately sabotaging a good idea. The clinics, which have eased pressure on EDs and provided much-needed extra health care in the regions, have been set up to fail. They bulk bill Medicare but because Medicare doesn't cover costs they are all losing money and are horribly understaffed for the job they're tasked to do. The question is *who* deliberately set them up to fall and *why*. It's not plausible that anyone could be so incompetent and there must be many people who know about this, so why haven't they been funded to at least cover costs? Or is this another plan to make the ALP look bad?

Yet Labor is its own worst enemy. The ALP and/or its bureaucracy are so busy putting up flawed and/or inadequate bills so they can wedge the Greens, that they avoid doing anything decent. They are a Right-wing party; often siding with the coalition. Why? Because the real rivals of the ALP are the Greens, and the real rivals of the L/NP are the 'teals'. Only the Greens and community independents threaten to take 'safe seats' from the Right-wing Liberal/Labor duopoly. That's why so many things the government does are aimed at making the Left of politics look bad or ineffective. They'd rather sell their soul to fascism than negotiate in good faith with the cross-benches. Arguably then, the community independents movement, minor parties and grass-roots politics are the key to breaking down the corporate-captured Liberal/Labor duopoly and getting them to divest their power back to the people.

We are going to need the best and brightest in our governments because the future holds challenges that our species has never faced before. I think the Westminster system needs major overhaul so that it's not just the leader of the party that wins the greater number of seats who gets to be the PM/leader of the country. Beyond getting the best leadership we need people who can rise above murderous militarism and think far smarter than the unjust, quasi-religious cult of market capitalism.

THE MARKET IS ANOTHER POCKET DEITY

As I explain elsewhere, our imagined gods come in all shapes and sizes. The more familiar ones are St Christopher medals for travellers and the usual range of charms that are thought to bring good outcomes. Then there are the semi-mythical yet real historical persons who people deify to the level of demigods, such as the Buddha, Jesus, and Muhammad. These are worshipped unquestionably by some, yet I would call them pocket-deities because they are conveniently-sized idols. As idols of the mind they allow us to avoid some of the work of thinking deeply about what these idols mean, or what the humans behind the myths were actually talking about. I argue that 'the Market' is another pocket-deity that a lot of people have come to idolise without any further thought. This idolatry of the market goes along with the love of money for its own sake and with capitalism as a global semi-religion that is meant to be the source of all meaning and value – and the reason for living for many people. As with other religions, the pocket deity is supposed to have magical powers of beneficence for its worshippers. One of those powers that you'll hear devotees of capitalism repeat to each other is the power to distribute goods most efficiently and fairly, but clearly 'the market' is failing to perform as claimed. When this pocket deity doesn't deliver, we call it a 'market failure', but when you start looking you see market failures everywhere. The market-deity really doesn't do miracles.

We could call the cost-of-living-crisis a market-failure, or we could also call it what it is: a deliberate piracy, a blatant theft from and punching-down on our most vulnerable and defenceless. The current cost-of-living difficulties are largely caused by greed-capitalism. Our governments simply lack the knowledge and iconoclastic confidence to defy the acolytes of marketism. However, as climate change is increasingly disrupting the generosity of the biosphere, all governments need to be a lot more brave and proactive.

A few of the many market failures in Australia are worth noting. The housing shortage and the degree of homelessness are obvious ones, and both these twins can be fixed by proactive government policies. A less frequently mentioned failure is that it's more expensive to live if you are poor than it is if you are wealthy. There are many ways this happens, but it's widely recognised now and it's called the 'poverty premium'. Even middle income earners are shocked by the unexplained price rises, and every Australian except the very wealthy feels that the rising cost of living has battered them. People are realising that ordinary consumers, we price-takers, have no control over how the market sets prices, or distributes goods and services, except to refuse to pay and walk away. There is also the 'pink tax' where most products that are uniquely for women and children (clothes, sanitary products, medications etcetera) are more expensive than for an adult male – often more than double the price! Another marketing nastiness (market failure) is 'shrinkflation' where goods are produced in smaller quantities, yet the price remains the same or higher. When and by whom will these practices be stopped? I'd argue that another market failure is the decades-long conversion of universities into profiteering businesses (with grossly overpaid CEOs/Vice Chancellors) instead of being institutions for the advancement of civilisation. Another market failure is the private–public health care split. Sadly, the privateers have hiked their prices while government support from Medicare has been deliberately neglected and not even indexed against the rocketing costs of medical care. With the studied neglect of Medicare, our health services have trended down to the horribly unequal America-style health system. Now, in Australia, the public have to wait for ages and/or be neglected while the wealthy get all the health benefits they ask for as soon as they can pay for them. But there were and are many things that our governments could have done and should be doing to remedy this failure.

More 'market failures' include wage-cost minimization practices like customer self-service. For example, supermarket self-check-outs, ATMs, telephone-answering bots, chat-bots, AI answering services that don't understand basic English yet never let you talk to a real human, and similar shite – just so that fewer people can be gainfully employed. There's the on-going erosion of services that used to employ people and the widespread closure of bank branches. Some banks no longer even provide cash for their customers. The many services that have been privatised are all pushing up their prices out of the reach of everyone except the very wealthy.

Meanwhile, the unemployment benefit is still only 39% of the minimum wage while the full-time minimum wage is still not enough for a family to live on. Added to which, many people can only get part-time or casual work, or else must work in the 'gig' economy where worker's rights are all but nonexistent. The sum of this is that Australia now has a large cohort of poverty-stricken unemployed and under-employed – the workless-poor and the working-poor. That this rich country allows such economic injustice, tolerates a rapidly rising cost-of-living with inflation far ahead of wages, and ignores business practices that amount to piracy should evoke both shame and rage among us all.

As mentioned before, Ben Chifley tried and failed to bring price controls under the power of the Commonwealth, and every legal re-try since then has also failed. But with our economy going exactly the wrong way, and while global heating is about to wreck the world's ability to produce food, every government, including the Australian Government, has plenty of reasons to proclaim ***an indefinite national emergency***, defy the high-priests of marketism, enact emergency powers in order to right these wrongs and pull our economies down into kindly and sustainable shape.

Such powers are vital now as we face the climate crisis: we have to try to restore Earth's energy balance. As discussed before, the temperature of the biosphere needs to stay in the relatively stable range that it's been in over our evolution. It's not just that CO_2 and CH_4 are helping to trap heat, but the heat has caused many effects that have slowed Earth's carbon-sinking capacity to a flat line! Our fear is that the air's percentage of oxygen will start to drop. If life on Earth is to survive we have to immediately stop habitat loss; plant trillions of trees; regenerate Nature at 'warp-speed'; cover every bare surface with plants or low-heat solar collectors; slow our pollution as fast as possible; contract our economy urgently, fairly, and with minimal suffering; make world peace and demilitarize the world before the year 2030; encourage a benign but rapid reduction of global populations; establish sustainable (zero fossil-fuel) agriculture, and do passive geo-engineering like turning every possible plant-free surface to a reflective white in order to restore Earth's albedo effect. It's an exhausting list, but all this must be done and done with only the minimal industrialisation needed to transition to sustainable living with 100% renewable energy.

Many people call global heating 'the climate crisis'. I don't like the term 'crisis' because it seems to imply a peak emergency that will fade as soon as the crisis is over. But global heating is not like that at all. The consequences of our failure to address the heating, from the 1980s and onward, may be present on Earth for thousands of years, if not longer. This is no mere crisis, this is the end of our world as we have known it. Our destructive, global, industrial, militarist, fossil-fueled economy is slowly killing the biosphere. It's happening slowly enough so that many people can ignore it, but it's happening so fast that Earth scientists and climate scientists are terrified. There are *so* many things we must do to keep our children from going extinct. Therefore, in the shadow of this hyperthreat to our existence, for our governments to enact emergency powers for some little things like prices and wages justification, well, this would seem a *very* small request.

THE JOB DESCRIPTION OF A CURRENCY

The reason for discussing money is that most of us use it every day and take it for granted, yet don't have a clear idea of what it is or how it works. Plus, describing how money works is to demonstrate that money is a public good and an indispensable tool. We also need to prove that it's the job of our government to make sure that our public money is doing its job for everyone fairly (and not being hoarded unfairly). But since the love of money has become an obsession, at least in developed nations, we should think about it in the hope of reducing some of the biosphere-destroying activities that are carried out in the pursuit of money. MMT argues correctly that it's important to discuss the nature and role of money so that we can successfully put it to work in any improved economic system. If money is to serve us well, then we need to be clear about what it is – and isn't – and how to make it work best for all.

Ever since civilization began, there have been forms of currency to facilitate the trade of goods and services as a way of keeping account of who owes what to whom. There is no doubt that money is, or should be, a public utility. It is a tool of accounting, and if it didn't exist in a hunter-gatherer society, then as soon as tribes started trading with each other a system of accounting for relative value would have had to be invented. Perhaps there's always been a quantum of 'money' in organised society. Associate Professor Steven Hail, and other experts in MMT, argue that money as we know it was invented by governments. This idea supports their argument that governments created taxation in order to create a demand for their fiat currency. But no doubt chieftains and kings found ways to bully goods and services out of underlings prior to modern taxation. And money has uses outside the spending and taxing circle of governments and the governed: the ordinary people needed a way to keep track of their trade, and that role of money as a public utility still exists. The fact that there are fewer traces of ancient money than might be expected could be explained by the proposition that various types of prehistoric money left no archaeological trace because they weren't as durable as the coins etc of our modern money are.

Early forms of money, like notched wooden tally sticks, date back at least 30,000 years. Clay tablets, and coins came later, but all were accounting tools. We can imagine early societies organising themselves and co-operating to share goods and services, and we can speculate that they each would have had some method of keeping account of the relative values of what each roaming band or tribe wanted to trade with another. Suffice to speculate that modern forms of money do the same job as when ochre was traded for shell necklaces, or hides were traded for spears. It's likely that ways of recording information, like writing and various forms of money all evolved together due to the need for organisation in societies. The reason I don't fully agree with MMT about all money being a government creation and fiefdom is because it could set some people against their government, and we need good governments that are at one with and serving the interests of all the people.

Most forms of money have had little or no intrinsic value, but some do. If a tradable good is used as a currency, it's called commodity money (anything from boomerangs to bottles of rum). Or the unit of exchange could represent something that has intrinsic value (e.g. a paper note that represents a pound of silver), so representative money is commodity-backed currency. Lastly, there is fiat money which has little intrinsic value but which is given a value by a king's fiat, decree, or government regulation. A currency could be both a representative and a fiat money; that's to say it could be pegged to something of value but enforced by fiat, edict, or regulation.

Printed paper money began in China during the Tang dynasty (618–907 CE), starting as merchants' receipts and becoming well established in the Yuan dynasty empire of Kublai Khan (1271–1368). It's said that when Marco Polo returned to Venice from China in 1295, Venetian people were astonished at Polo's description of how this legal tender was enforced by Kublai Khan as a fiat currency. (In 1971, US President Nixon ended the convertibility of the US dollar to gold, effectively ending the Bretton Woods System. After that, most currencies were fiat currencies, but most also opted for a floating exchange rate set by Foreign Exchange [Forex] markets. More on this later.)

During the colonial period, the colonizers, including imperialist exploiters like the East India Company, wanted to extort labour and goods out of indigenous populations, so they either imposed slavery or else they imposed a tax and payment system that required the locals to earn the 'coin' to pay the tax. Money was again a way to account for the value of the labour and goods being shifted. It was a proxy for value. Spending money is just using the proxy to get what you want, and earning money is just providing services and/or goods in order to get the proxy money for further use. Either way, the proxy has to be exchanged (circulated) in order for it to be of use.

Hoarding money (earned or not) renders that money useless because it means that the *value* is not being circulated. Bloated billionaire bank accounts and large numbers recorded in tax-haven accounts, may appear to be harmless numbers but they could be recycled through other accounts in order to do many good things – let your imagination dwell on that. People like Larry Fink, Elon Musk, Jeff Bezos and others could do *so* much for *so* many people, but all they want is to increase their own profit and power.

When banks or governments create too much money, they are just devaluing those proxy symbols of real value. Taxation and the legal system that backs it are the means by which powers bully value out of their society (with threats of violence/jail). Many will not like to be coerced out of their money, but I argue that wherever money lies stagnant it is failing to do its job; therefore, governments should tax the mega-rich much more than at present. As the saying goes, 'For the love of money is the root of all evil': (1 Timothy 6:9–11)

Since money was always an accounting system (where the measure-units [e.g. dollars] mostly had little or no intrinsic value but were essentially a tradable IOU used for keeping account of the transfer of value), then what is the good of our floating currency system where our units of account don't even have a fixed representational value? Yet that's what the international financial system is using ever since Nixon ended the gold standard. The relative transnational purchasing power of our money depends on the whims of the [pro-American] money markets to set those relative values for the global currencies. Of course, the markets privilege the American dollar and give it the highest purchasing power. Sadly, countries that have bought American dollars, or traded their produce for US dollars, are reluctant to end the privileging of the USD as the world's 'reserve currency'. This superior purchasing power gives the US a massive 'house-edge' that effectively imports real wealth into the US as the US exports US dollars. But if that privilege did end, then much of the International wealth flowing to the US would stop, and any (surviving) US government would have to care more for the people rather than using that wealth to practice militarism and make wars. For example, the US spends as much on their nuclear weapons as every other Nuke-armed country combined, and the flow of money to the US means that international wealth is paying for the utter waste that is US militarism.

To return to the job description of a currency, the quantity of 'coin' available needs to be theoretically limitless but practically kept limited so the currency doesn't fail in its primary role. The role of money, firstly, is to be a light-weight, easily-carried representation of an agreed value. Secondly, money (like blood in a body) has to circulate in order to do its job of transporting value and thirdly, any form of money should be able to act as a virtual store of value; i.e. an agreed value for which people are willing to trade their goods or labour. So, the job-description of a currency is to represent value, circulate value, and store value.

As described earlier, the so-called 'taxpayer's money' is really the public's money because it is issued by our government to do its job for society. If the value of a currency cannot be agreed upon reliably over time, then the currency starts to fail at its job-description. That's why 'crypto-currencies', whose value fluctuates widely with the 'crypto' market, are not real currencies because they do not do the job expected of money; rather, they're a speculator's play-thing, not a reliable exchange-medium, reward for labour, facilitator of trade, or store of value. In fact crypto coins are all a con man's Ponzi scheme – trading a fancy chimera for real currency and inflating it up like the price of tulips during Tulip Mania (1634–1637). Although many people will have invested in this speculation, and large amounts of computer energy will have been burned in creating the crypto numbers, and maybe some people (e.g. Trump/Musk followers) will have become rich along the way, ultimately it will be seen that there's nothing of value underneath this long-running crypto-bubble and many people will have lost out to the con-men.

Obviously, any level of inflation sees a currency starting to fail at its jobs of representation and storage, and the higher the inflation the worse the money is in failure. Hyperinflation is when a currency completely fails at its job description. So, instead of allowing any level of avoidable inflation (to give business a house-edge), our Federal Government and our Reserve Bank should act as one in quashing the cycle of price-rises and the erosion of the utility of our currency – not by raising interest rates but by doing all the positive regulation that any healthy body/economy should be doing. Apart from its many other jobs – being the brains of the outfit etc – the government has to be the heart that pumps the blood (currency) around the economy; i.e. it has to ***spend and tax***. Spending and taxing are primary jobs of any effective government – judiciously, of course.

Despite those dual roles of government (heart and mind), the body analogy does not imply a centrist system. Rather, the system/economy is a grass-roots democracy whose raison d'être is to serve the will of every citizen/cell and answer their genuine needs – something that the free-market, laissez faire government in Canberra, and Neoliberal economics more broadly, are seriously failing to do.

Price-gouging – again

Contrary to the RBA's fanciful 'wage-price spiral', the substantially increased profits of many corporations has proven that their price-gouging has encouraged only more price-gouging, which has caused a 'profit-price spiral'. Consequently, inflation peaked at over 7% p.a. and has been reluctant to slow. This is because the RBA's interest rate rises mainly hurt those whose income level constrains them from either saving or spending while advantaging those who have money to spend – thereby encouraging further rounds of profit-seeking and unfair price-rises, *aka* price gouging. Anyone shopping at Woolworths or Coles will tell you that this duopoly has been raising their prices far more than is justified.

And it's not just the big corporations that are marking up their prices just because there is an expectation of price increases (so-called inbuilt inflation – inflation stoking inflation). On the 7th of February 2024, Professor Allan Fels AO released the report into the cost of living and price gouging that he had been commissioned to complete by the ACTU. He confirmed what we all knew from personal observation over many months.

> https://www.abc.net.au/news/2024-02-07/allan-fels-price-gouging-report-cost-of-living-crisis/103431866

Also, companies have been indexing their price rises against inflation, raising prices against price rises. Added to that, on 1st of July 2023, power prices went up across most states by a massive 10–20% for NO publicly known reason! Such rabid greed is a 'market failure'. As Adam Smith is thought to have said: *All for ourselves, and nothing for other people, seems, in every age of the world, to have been the **vile maxim** of the masters of mankind.*

THE DEFICIT MYTH, BUDGET DEFICIT OR SURPLUS AND AUSTERITY

The 2020 book *The Deficit Myth* by Stephanie Kelton describes the banking situation in the United States of America and points out that a government that issues its own fiat currency does not have to manage and balance a budget like a household budget; it can 'create' as much money as it needs. This popular misconception, that the budget of a currency issuing government is the same as a household budget, has been very persistent for a very long time. Although it was known before, the power of deficit spending was shown by the success of Roosevelt's New Deal. A government budget surplus is not necessarily a bad thing, but it is meaningless, stupid and useless while-ever there is work that our public money should be doing – like curing poverty, building affordable homes, or solving any of our other problems.

The Labor government announced budget surpluses in May 2023 and in May 2024, yet they have continued the mean austerity policies that characterised the previous (L/NP) regime. With the tiny exceptions of a few scraps for Jobseekers and a few dollars more in rent assistance, the ALP continued the Right-wing policies of the L/NP. Treasurer Chalmer's budget of May 9th 2023 was like rubbing our noses in excreta with its arrogant disdain for the underprivileged. A paltry $20 a week extra for Jobseekers who are far below the official poverty line and $15.50 a week extra in rent assistance when landlords are charging many hundreds of dollars extra per week in rent, are insulting numbers. The economist Peter Martin dryly noted that these tiny increases were at 'homeopathic' doses. Yet some out-of-touch economists claimed these might still push up prices and cause the RBA to raise interest rates again. Before September 2024 was over Labor Treasurer Chalmers announced another unnecessary budget surplus ($15.8 billion) again without curing the poverty of those on Jobseeker allowance and similar payments, nor addressing the malnutrition among the poor as the food charities and food banks in Australia reported doubling of demand for their free food. What is even more infuriating is that members of the L/NP opposition have the gall to tell sickening lies to the effect that ending this parsimony for those suffering real poverty is somehow an attack on the pockets of the middle class. Outrageous nonsense!

MORTGAGE STRESS

In the 2022–2023 episode, when interest rates were raised as fast as the RBA could plausibly raise them, people struggled to pay the extra money to the banks. Consequently, approximately 500,000 home buyers suffered mortgage stress, and mortgage defaults increased. Sharply rising interest rates caused a fall in house prices, so home buyers who bought at the peak of the market, with low-interest loans in the short term, got stuck with sharply rising mortgages on houses they couldn't sell easily. It's called a 'mortgage prison'. For the sake of reducing the financial damage to home buyers and businesses, interest rates must be lowered again as fast as they were raised. This is because:

  a the financial anxiety of mortgage stress is a genuine form of mental-health suffering, and
  b because more money going to the private banks does NOT stop the price-setters from gouging their customers – also known as inflation.

The sooner there are people on the RBA board who will loudly and effectively ridicule Monetarism and its current lies – e.g. that NAIRU actually exists, or that jacking up mortgages slows price-hikes, or that inflation at any level is a good thing – the better! Plus, if you doubt that the commercial banks are privateers, legal pirates, then watch this important video by Alan Kohler. It may need several viewings to become clear:

https://www.youtube.com/watch?v=iYUlkPa02f0&t=3s

UNAFFORDABLE HOUSING

As Alan Kohler has suggested, Australia's emerging recession is not so much an unemployment recession as a homelessness recession. In November 2023, the *Quarterly Essay* published a thorough examination by Mr. Kohler of this exact problem. His long essay was entitled *The Great Divide*. It is well worth reading. In short, Alan Kohler suggests an 'all of the above' (or even any) national approach to housing policy where argument and inaction have been the norm. Of course Australia's government should have intervened in the housing market years ago, but the prospect of an asset and investment class that was as safe as property for wealth gain was far too tempting for too many people and politicians alike. Consequently, the split between those who could afford to buy a home in the past and those who cannot afford one now has become an unbridgeable chasm.

Housing was allowed to become unaffordable:

  a because there's been no intervention in the runaway property bubble that rocketed the price of home-ownership

- b because no government has had the courage to intervene in the 'holy market' and stop property owners getting big increases in their wealth(soft tax on capital gains)
- c because landlords have been getting very nice tax write-offs through 'negative gearing' for their investment properties, plus gouging tenants with unjustified and savage rent increases, and
- d because the many governments in Australia have not taken responsibility for ensuring an adequate supply of affordable new homes, especially not enough for the high number of workers they are importing from other countries.

It's both a supply and a demand problem. To fix this, the government must:

- a pour vastly more money into genuinely creating homes (not just their present 'Future Fund')
- b increase urban population density instead of alienating more farmland
- c greatly increase (electrified) public transport and all other urban and regional services
- d put price controls on all forms of housing
- e strictly control rent increases by putting them under the power of the proposed Prices and Salaries Justification Authority
- f reverse privatisation by compulsorily buying back Toll roads that make urban living untenable and make all roads free again
- g institute fuel rationing, efficiency standards and other incentives to reduce commuter traffic and enable people to live where they work, and
- h improve all public transport (electric buses & trains) and make fares supercheap.

There is another consideration about housing, and that is to build to standards that will be disaster resistant. Many of us will consider moving underground to some degree. Since flash-floods, blizzards, tornadoes, super-storms, giant hail, bushfires, and severe heatwaves can all be expected to be more severe and sudden, then we must build our homes with a mind to expecting the unexpected.

RENT-RISE CRISIS

Rent-gouging landlords are not mythical. Of course there are many good landlords who want to be fair, but ever since homes (property) were deliberately turned into a booming asset class, those who could find the money to invest in it were given leave to be as greedy as their personal morality would allow. In an ideal world there would be no landlords because everyone who needed their own home would either own it already or else be on an easy hire-purchase scheme toward owning it. But about one third of Australians are renting – which means there are a large number of landlords too, so renting won't vanish anytime soon. Given it's a necessary evil (for now) rent costs and conditions *must* be regulated.

Government policies ordain high population growth, especially through high immigration levels. The easy path to migration has been very biased towards the fortunate, the wealthy and the well educated; it is quite the opposite for asylum-seekers and refugees. High immigration was, and is, being used to pump-up GDP growth numbers and keep unemployment high enough to suppress wages. Due to the demand for GDP growth, the large number of people arriving has surpassed our capacity to build new homes for them, so the competition for homes has grown to a disastrous degree. We are near the point where only the very wealthy can afford a home. Homelessness is growing. People are living in temporary accommodation, reduced to cars, tents, or even sleeping rough. Australia now has its own sui-generis, internally-displaced refugees. It's another failure of the market, and it's leaving far too many people uncertain about having a home to live in.

This can partly be fixed by government-imposed rent-setting rules and standards, and by referring rents to the Prices and Wages Justification Authority. But demand for homes still exceeds supply. So governments have to build homes as fast as possible (smaller, more disaster-proof homes, preferably). And the federal government needs to build social housing instead of leaving it to private developers or the cash-strapped states. Plus we need to fill all the homes that are currently empty, initiate a hire-purchase scheme for public housing, and increase population densities by building smaller and taller housing in the cities. As said earlier, we need to improve public transport by having fewer big cars, many smaller electric vehicles, plus more electric buses and trains. We do NOT need more planes (until they're electric) or airports because they add too much to global heating. We also need to provide much better services in regional and rural areas where people would live if they could. This means incentivising many more doctors, teachers, and all other service-providers into country towns and remote communities from which they've been drained – often by the exact same market forces that the irresponsible, laissez-faire governments have unleashed. The federal government could also focus on better immigration support (and asylum-seeker settlement) aimed at enabling the well-being of all immigrants and all our people, rather than merely jacking-up the GDP numbers. This would mean slowing business migration in favour of professionals, trade-workers, (although educating existing residents would be better), family reunions, giving permanency to those on uncertain visas, and settling those who are Australia's responsibility already as 'immigration detainees', i.e. our political prisoners.

HOMELESSNESS IN AUSTRALIA

As stated above, homelessness is growing in a country where this should never be the case. An estimated 122,500 Australians experienced homelessness in 2023, but this may be a gross under-estimate due to the difficulty identifying the homeless and the thousands who are still living in temporary accommodation due to climate-related disasters – i.e. the fires and floods since 2019. Many of the homeless are women in their later years who do not have the financial privilege of affording a home, even if they once did. Both state and federal governments have been derelict in their response to the need to house everyone in safety, and they have too often made excuses and blamed each other for laziness and inaction. The previous L/NP regime was criminally negligent. For example, Morrison promised the victims of 'the 2019–2020 Summer of Fires' $2 billion dollars for recovery, but when a share was sought by fire-victims the federal bureaucrats told them it was 'notional' – that's to say, non-existent! But people should also be angry at the current ALP government that it can promise America's Military-Industrial Complex $368 billion (or whatever) for nuclear submarines we don't need, but fail to tax the fossil fuel companies properly. The ALP government plans to spend only about $0.5 billion annually for safe and affordable homes when the need demands ten times that amount. Our government could buy back large numbers of 'investment properties' and resell them by hire-purchase, as mentioned above. They could help building companies that are failing for a multitude of reasons, and they could establish a national public builder that actually builds affordable homes. They could also crack down on rent-gouging landlords, and increase welfare payments to adequate levels. But at present the federal government is only offering a 'help to buy' scheme that is so limited and so poorly structured that almost nobody will be able to use it.

A report from Homelessness Australia released on the 18th November 2024 said there could be three million Australians on the verge of homelessness. The study found that the number of people at risk had grown 63%, overwhelming the ability of services to help them. Many services have had to turn away people desperately needing help. This includes women and children fleeing domestic violence. It doesn't have to be this way.

In a press release from ACT independent Senator David Pocock we learn that the ALP government actually opposes legislating a plan to fix the housing and homelessness problem in Australia. A government-dominated senate committee is proposing to block a joint bill from Senator Pocock and the Member for North Sydney, Kylea Tink MP that seeks to legislate a rolling 10-year national housing and homelessness plan. Senator Pocock says it's extraordinary that Australia doesn't have a National Housing and Homelessness Plan, and even more extraordinary that the ALP government says legislating such a plan is unnecessary, contrary to the weight of evidence tendered to the committee. Perhaps there are some wrecking-crew politicians or wrecking-crew bureaucrats involved.

Former Labor Senator for NSW, Doug Cameron, has been advocating for modular-housing in all parts of Australia. Mr Cameron says modular housing could provide a practical solution to our housing needs. Mr Cameron said:

> *My preference would be that we invest in a strong modular housing industry. ... If you use modular housing, you are building in factories, creating modern homes that are cheaper to cool, cheaper to heat, delivered quickly, not affected by bad weather, and can massively support the existing building industry.*

Former Senator Cameron has been a strong advocate of the benefits of modular housing as it is done in Europe. He expressed frustration with current government spending, suggesting that public money could be better spent on housing than on the military. Mr Cameron said:

> *At the moment, we're too busy investing in nuclear submarines and maintaining the status quo ... I think we need to gain some wisdom and start looking at what is important for Australians: providing affordable, safe housing that can offer them and their families a future.*

Doug Cameron also wrote:

> *The renowned Oxford philosopher Isaiah Berlin said: "Freedom for the wolves has often meant death to the sheep". The wolves are freely gorging on the victims of the housing 'market'. The market cannot solve the housing crisis. Fiddling with market solutions will not work.*

Safe and affordable homes must be regarded as a human right. The market failure caused by seeing homes only as an asset-class for profiteering must be corrected as soon as possible.

MEDIOCRE ALP

As stated earlier, the federal ALP government has had a mixed record since May 2022. They have done many good things, but not enough, and done far too many negative things as well. This essay will seem too critical of federal Labor; that's not because they are the worst but because the expectations of them were so high after we finally got rid of the neo-fascist regime of Scummo and Co. Sadly, the ALP has not lived up to our hopes. It's regrettable that so many good ALP politicians toe the party line. When I learnt to shear sheep I also learnt how the ALP grew out of the shearer's strike of 1891, so I know how the rule of party solidarity was essential to the struggle for workers' rights against powerful capitalists. But it's no longer useful in today's struggle for reason and for truth itself. Senator Fatima Payman held this up to the light regarding the destruction of Gaza. The ALP was trying to be diplomatic and not upset any faith community, but the Right-wing media were actively subverting the truth about the pro-peace ***anti-Zionist*** protests by pretending they were actually ***anti-Semitic***, which they were not! The deliberate, sly conflation of these two totally different mind-sets should have been called out by our leaders long ago.

I have no problem with Jewish people – they are just people with just another religion. What I do have a problem with is anyone who bullies anyone else or kills anyone else for selfish reasons. The Zionists have bullied the Palestinians for at least 76 years – as long as the state of Israel has existed. And the Palestinians have fought back, as you would expect any displaced people to do. We can condemn the brutality and murdering of both sides, but we can't pretend that either side is morally superior to the other. It's just that the Zionists wanted the land that belonged to the Palestinians and the Palestinians have never wanted to give away their homeland. Europe's Jewish refugees certainly deserved better treatment after the Nazis attempted genocide of them in the 1940s, but that can never excuse the attempted genocide of the Palestinian people by Zionist Israeli people.

The ALP has been trying to sit on the fence on this issue, but instead of letting the far-Right and the News Corp/L/NP nexus to falsely conflate anti-Zionism with anti-Semitism the federal government should have taken the lead in denouncing this lie. Only people with very limited historical knowledge would confuse those two sentiments, and only the very young could think that the Zionist vs. Hamas conflict started on 7th October 2023. To be opposed to the ultra-violence and war crimes of Netanyahu's army is NOT being anti-Semitic, it is being pro-humanity, pro-life, and anti-genocide.

The worst crime of any of Australia's governments is not taking global heating seriously enough. We should have been taking it seriously decades ago, but although the ALP says they care, they are still allowing more coal and gas expansion. We don't expect the L/NP to take climate science seriously – they're still on the level of the chimp who called himself 'Scomo' and waved a piece of lacquered coal around in Parliament while the other chimps laughed. Many in the ALP know better yet won't get tough about global heating. They let the Murdoch media cast doubt on climate science and haven't had the courage to hold a media Royal Commission even though Kevin Rudd garnered half a million signatures in a petition calling for just that. In January 2023 there was a burst of publicity that told the world Exonn Mobil knew the dangers of climate change in 1977 but later denied it.

The ALP can and should be taking much more serious action on global heating and fixing the cost of living much better too. The two are linked and the former is going to make the latter worse no matter what – and a lot worse if we don't fix our whole economic system.

And yes, I'm critical of the Greens party too, because like any team or group they can fall into tribalism, group-think and a sort of cultural conformity that stultifies a group. That is part of the reason why the L/NP and News Corp have fallen into their own echo-chamber of deluded neo-Fascism – they only ever talk to each other and confirm their own biases. It may also be why the ALP has more in common with the L/NP than with anyone on the cross-bench – the politicians of those parties are obliged to see and hear too much of each other, and they get sucked into group-think.

Of course The Greens are focused on trying to get enough members elected so they can form a Green (survival-focused) government. Therefore, they dare not speak out as strongly as they would like to (or I would like them to), about global heating in particular, because it frightens the uncommitted and unengaged voters. The rivalry for votes between the ALP and Greens has caused the ALP to refuse to co-operate with The Greens and to seek support from the far-Right L/NP instead. This just shows how cowed the ALP has become that they'd rather play footsy with the Fascists than to face down the far-Right, pro-American, anti-life News Corp. Some people complain that The Greens are too strident, too self-righteous, and too middle-class or bourgeois, but even their critics have to admit that The Greens are at least the most socially compassionate, future-focused, economics-literate and science-literate party currently in politics.

There are millions of people who are far more clever than I am, but somehow their voices are muted. Some folks will label me as a Green, or a Trotsky socialist, but Trotsky was murdered in 1940 by one of Stalin's death squads (a crime reprised in recent years), so the notion of revolution is long dead. Anyway, if revolution sinks to violence it has failed already. I must emphasise that my economic ideas are NOT communism but survivalism. Sustainable peace needs all 'sides' to move towards co-operation, even if agreeing to disagree. I prefer a Fabian-style cultural evolution that's focused on restoration. I'd claim to be more radical than most Greens, and instead would claim to be a Survivalist.

I'm most critical of the dregs of the federal L/NP regime. Very few in the L/NP are people of good intention, or have a sincere desire to do good for Australians. Bridget Archer is an honourable exception. It is my honest opinion that the current L/NP federal team is just a mob of deliberately-ignorant, science-denying, selfish people who team up with News Corp to promote Trumpist, lying, pro-American, pro-war stupidity, and to deceive as many people as they can. They can never be trusted with government again.

All the very many News Corp outlets in Australia, like Sky (so-called) News, act as propaganda machines for the far-Right L/NP, just as News Corp's Fox News works tirelessly for the apparently crazy US Republican Party. One example is when the L/NP announced a fantasy to build seven nuclear power plants around Australia over coming decades. The American Murdoch-owned News Corp backed it to the hilt even though the Nukes would be too expensive, too slow to build, too unsafe, too under-performing, and produce much more radioactive waste than the L/NP claimed. Either they all knew these facts or else they were criminally ignorant. If they weren't that ignorant then they were certainly lying and spreading disinformation. Their lies must be called out for the good of the country. The L/NP's nuclear plan is obviously just an effort to stop the transition to cheap renewable energy, to continue the burning of coal and gas, and to build a nuclear industry to support America's plans for nuclear war against Australia's biggest trading partner. The only goal of the L/NP is political power and access to the corporate-capitalist money-trough.

The Murdoch media and others are creating social division in Australia because it's their business model. They lie and roll out their nasty venom creating a sense of them-and-us in the country, but we not only do we not need that destruction of social cohesion, but their behaviour is also an attack on our chances of survival which is more dangerous than anything external to Australia. The divisive, far-Right media are 'an enemy within', and the ALP should have the courage to call them out.

One major achievement to which the ALP contributed was that on 26th June 2024, the Australian publisher Julian Assange was finally saved from America's lethal revenge for WikiLeaks having exposed US war crimes. The ALP had apparently worked for Assange's rescue in secret, but it took a lot of pressure and work from a lot of other people, his family and a very dedicated legal team, and it nearly didn't happen. Sadly, almost simultaneously the Environment minister gave the go-ahead for Senex Energy (jointly owned by South Korea's steel company, Posco, and Gina Rinehart) to develop and operate up to 151 new coal seam gas-fracking wells in inland Queensland. The Australia Institute's Rod Campbell said: "While Australia is distracted talking about the L/NP nuclear charade, the federal government is approving new fossil fuel projects." (When the IPCC says there should be zero new fossil fuel projects.) And the Lock the Gate Alliance accused the coal seam gas industry of "irreversibly damaging Queensland's best farmland". Also in the same week the ALP teamed up with the (apparently child-hating) L/NP *again* to defeat a bill that would have applied a '***Duty of Care***', for future generations, upon federal ministerial decisions.

Australians learnt to have low expectations of the L/NP regime, but the federal ALP has shaken even the modest expectations we had of them. ACOSS has shown that the real value of income support payments have been reduced for decades, as neoliberal economics demands, but the ALP has only added tiny extras of no significance. To say they are out of touch is a radical understatement. They could double the Jobseeker allowance (as was done during the first Covid crisis) and still only bring it up to the poverty line. By making such small, often token efforts to fix poverty, inequality, unaffordable housing, homelessness, inflation, the cost-of-living, and all the other social injustices that have built up in Australia, the Labor Party has confirmed it's a Rightist party. They've been very weak on environmental protection and stupidly and stubbornly averse to accepting good suggestions and/or amendments from the cross benches. The ALP has also colluded with the L/NP too often for accusations of duopoly, or monopoly, to be refuted. Corporate-captured and timid, they've allowed fossil fuel expansions and new projects when zero was the correct number. They haven't stopped native forest logging, yet have also turned a blind eye to the fraudulent aspects of the Carbon Credit Scheme. Australia was turned into a quasi-fascist plutocracy by the L/NP, but the ALP has not fixed that yet. The Labor government has continued with the economic, strategic and foreign-policy blunder that is AUKUS. They've let the US military reduce Australia to an American military asset via the Force Posture Agreement (see AUSMIN July 2023). And they're *giving* over $4 billion AUD to the US Navy Submarine-building program (and that's ***not*** counting AUKUS payments). The ALP government will also give billions of dollars to the UK submarine industry.

We don't need any of this expensive war-making nonsense because while the American mentality is seeking the latest 'enemy' to justify their war economy, the issue that engages the Communist Party of China is how to make life good for their people so they can stay in power. They are not going to invade Australia because they know they can't push Australia's production any more than foreign and Australian-owned corporations already are. Plus, clever Chinese observers will have noted that we Australians are pushing this big desert-island continent far beyond its limits anyway. We have extracted more water from our rivers than Nature can replace; if an agricultural region looks like it has gas or coal beneath it then our rapacious fossil-fuel corporations will drill it or dig it up (e.g. the black soil of the Liverpool Plains or the Hunter Valley); there is nowhere that our profiteers are leaving something for any future generation, so why would any other nation want to invade this excoriated, bushfire-prone, miner's rubble-heap of a country?

Please don't misunderstand me, I love Australia and there are still a few tiny gems of beauty hidden where the mining industry or forest-destroying industries have not been able to see an easily-extracted mega-profit, but the popular misconception that other countries are envious of our mineral resources and our open spaces is nothing but a Furphy. None of our remote regions are fully habitable because there are not enough plants to the support rain and water cycle, and not enough rain to support the plants with adequate water cycle.

In consideration of Australia's military needs, our geo-political security, and where we should invest our resources, I refer you to one of Australia's wisest 'elders' in these matters: John Menadue AO, who was born in 1935. He is the Founder and Editor in Chief of the independent journal *Pearls and Irritations*. He was a former Secretary of the Department of Prime Minister and Cabinet under Gough Whitlam and Malcolm Fraser, Ambassador to Japan, Secretary of the Department of Immigration, and CEO of Qantas. The wide-ranging discussion below was published in August 2024, and in my opinion it is a vitally important warning for Australia. Mr. Menadue is disappointed with the federal Labor government, due to its timidity. He is also deeply sceptical of the AUKUS arrangement and concerned that Australia is sacrificing both our security and our sovereignty as we become inextricably dominated by the American military-business complex. Even before the outrageous return of D. J. Trump to the position of POTUS, John Menadue said of the United States: *America is the most violent, aggressive country in the world.* and *The greatest threat to peace in the world is the United States.* Please read this article:

> https://johnmenadue.com/if-we-have-strong-leadership-we-can-break-from-the-united-states/

Sadly, the ALP federal government is still cruelly mistreating asylum seekers with off-shore imprisonment and ***needlessly*** pursuing 'debts' from welfare recipients with the same flawed logic and classist, punching-down intent that underpinned the deadly Robodebt scam. Plus, the Australian Tax Office is equally needlessly chasing dubious old tax debts, notably on small businesses, so the number of insolvencies has risen sharply. Insolvencies among building companies are at a crisis level. This at a time when we need all the building we can get, due to the intersection of government housing policies and immigration policies, yet the federal housing minister seems fixated on establishing an unnecessary $10 billion 'future fund'. Bankruptcy among builders has been partly due to rapid inflation in materials costs, but also partly due to high interest rates. (Thanks, RBA.) Plus, although the ALP did modify the original Stage 3 tax cuts, they were still too generous to the very wealthy (us 'boomers' and the highly paid), which again widened intergenerational inequality and recklessly stoked inflation up again. None of this has to be this way.

The ALP has not stopped deforestation through native forest logging and has reused the old excuse that it's a state responsibility. It would be better for everyone if all loggers were paid sit-down money rather than kill another tree. Better still would be if 1% of loggers felled plantation trees onl, while the other 99% were re-employed to plant a hundred trees for every one felled. The federal government is defending carbon credits that have been shown to be worthless, yet they're okay about climate protest being criminalised.

In an address to the Business Council of Australia on 17th September 2024, Anthony Albanese accused the Greens of "gesture-based climate amendments" for wanting to put a 'climate trigger' (i.e. considering global heating when deciding projects) into Labor's legislation for an Environmental Protection Agency. That insult to all climate-science literate Australians was about as low and stupid as coal-waving Scummo might have gone.

The community independents movement aims to install locally-focused representatives in Australia's parliament rather than deliberately-ignorant major-party hacks. This movement is gaining popularity and had some success in electing the so-called 'teal' independents in 2022. Of course the major party Liberal/Labor duopoly is doing everything it can to make democracy difficult for those independents. Both the old parties were shaken by the success of independent candidates. These candidates campaigned successfully on the three big issues of the time: gender equity for women, integrity/openness in government, and, most of all, trying to promote government action on climate change. Anthony Albanese became prime minister mostly because he wasn't the completely ridiculous 'Scumo'. That will not help him or the federal ALP in 2025.

The federal Labor government is still favouring rich religious schools over public education as the L/NP did. They have not stopped prosecuting whistle-blowers like ATO truth-teller, Richard Boyle, and the government is no more transparent than it was under the last regime.

Australians are justifiably worried because anti-egalitarian, over-privileged, plutocratic power-elites have established themselves permanently as the ruling class in Australia's politics, in our public service, and in our media. There is crony and relational corruption, or nepotism, grey corruption and even criminal corruption enabling the maintenance of these political and corporate elites, and the major-party duopoly too often behaves like a monopoly.

Sadly, the ALP is failing many people's expectation that they'd expunge and prosecute all the deeply corrupt people from the L/NP regime. No one has been prosecuted over Robodebt even though the

National Anti-Corruption Commission (NACC) was given evidence by the Robodebt Royal Commission. And the only people to be prosecuted for other corruption, and even for murders by Australian soldiers, have been the whistleblowers.

As mentioned above, much to the disappointment of its supporters, the ALP has maintained the serious level of poverty in Australia. Homelessness has scarcely been touched, health and education remain poorly funded while Defence Minister Marles throws hundreds of billions of dollars at AUKUS and is set to fulfill Peter Dutton's 2022 commitment to spend $3.5 billion on another military extravagance, i.e. 75 new M1A2 Abrams tanks. (Just *what* is one quarter of a tank division going to defend in the vastness of the Australian continent?) Meanwhile the government says it can't afford any more money for essential services.

As ABC political correspondent Laura Tingle politely said of the budget surplus in May 2023:

> *It's a pretty bad political look to have a huge surplus and to not have made some structural spending decisions in core Labor areas to address years of Coalition parsimony.*

This remained acutely true when Treasurer Chalmers announced a $22.1 billion dollar budget surplus in September 2023, and acutely true again when the Treasurer handed down another needless budget surplus of $15.8 billion in September 2024, yet **still** kept unemployed people in poverty. In 2024 Dr Chalmers added $300 per household (regardless of how rich or poor they may be) for energy bills and a token boost to rent assistance. Meanwhile, even the *revised* Stage 3 Tax Cuts for the rich were very inflationary. During much of 2024 the 'sticky' inflation caused the RBA to talk about more interest rate rises. And even though unemployment rose in June 2024, it wasn't enough damage to satisfy RBA governor Bullock. The fact that 50,000 extra jobs were created that month had the RBA threatening a 14th rise in interest rates. As mentioned, our Treasurer might have given away his power to veto that, but fortunately in August 2024 he decided to keep the treasurer's veto.

Following each Labor budget, the Opposition and some economists claimed that the minuscule "cost of living relief" was going to push up prices. It is mind boggling that these petty nouveau-aristocrats have the hide to say that curing poverty is inflationary. How can enabling unemployed people to eat healthily and pay some bills possibly cause cost-push, demand-pull, or even price-gouging price-hikes? Laughable, of course! Only when that money flows to the big-spenders can it incentivise price-setters to mark up prices. And some of the same petty-aristocrats have the gall to mouth the term 'politics of envy' when anyone questions their seemingly endless self-serving greed. What the poor or the 'average battlers' feel is very rarely envy but always deep *rage* against economic injustice.

Workers know when injustice is at large. A cleaner who works hard for 60 hours a week, but still can't take home a fair wage, will recognise the injustice of a public servant who takes home nearly a million dollars per year for making bad decisions randomly, or a CEO who takes home multi-millions for sacking people, out-sourcing labour, putting profit before safety, and trashing the reputation of the company (e.g. QANTAS). That's injustice, and those who say the workers are envious have got it wrong. Injustice doesn't cause envy – it causes fury.

The ALP (of which I was a member for 5 years) is backing the wrong horse. The federal ALP seems to be making the greatest mistake in the entire post-invasion (1788) history of our nation by backing the far-Right super-coalition that's made up of the US Military Industrial Complex, the racist and openly Sinophobic News Corp, the Dutton-led and Trump-inspired neo-fascist L/NP, the fossil-fuel corporations, and the murdering, genocidal, Netanyahu-led, Apartheid-colonialist, land-thieving Zionist lobby. That mega-coalition is set against almost every other country in the world, including the peace-making arm of the United Nations. The Labor Party needs to be supporting the human rights of the world's majority against American-empowered militarism and war-making. Added to that, the ALP needs to get scientifically rational about the hyperthreat of global heating and stop allowing the fossil fuel corporations to keep growing. (Santos had Scumo for that.) We can't expect anything but lies from the L/NP/News Corp COALition so the ALP has to grow a spine. Labor should fear the tsunami of disappointment they are building up behind them.

WAGES AND WELFARE

It must be stated that the only reason employers and workers ever made an agreement for payment for the labour (or intellectual efforts) of the worker, was so the employer could gain the *surplus value* of the worker's labour and so the worker could get fair value from exchanging their labour. No worker would not have sold their labour for wages and conditions if there was any opportunity to obtain a fair exchange in any less subservient way. The net gain always goes to the employer, not the worker, so if anyone should be humble and grateful for employment it's the employer, not the worker. Sadly, neoliberalism, through reinstating 19th century slave-wages and poor conditions, has returned virtual slavery to many countries. So we will need unions while ever there are employers. If you don't like unions (although I do), then you have to get rid of employers first. Few enjoy conflict between workers and employer-owner-bosses, so the best way to fix that is to turn workers into the genuine owners of enterprise (*not* via soviet-style state ownership). Where there are government (state) owned sectors of natural monopolies, like health and education, we will still need public service unions to ensure that public servants get fair pay and conditions.

When a worker is unemployed (full employment means everyone who wants a job has one, and the government can guarantee that), they should be paid a living retainer so that they and their family do not suffer poverty. This would not cause laziness (or what's termed 'welfarism') because just as share-bludgers keep themselves physically and economically active, so do the so-called dole-bludgers. Rather, when everyone is guaranteed an income of their choice (either meaningful employment or personal creativity), this liberates everyone to do the kind of activity they feel is of greatest value and reward to them. This would not only add to Gross National Happiness, but also lift the richness of our societies in many ways. For example, a person on 'welfare' might choose to grow a food garden, produce great music or art, or perhaps study in their field of greatest interest. Alternatively, another person who has gained a good free education might choose to serve as a carer for the aged or as a doctor or teacher. When the greatest number of people are fairly employed at what they like, then society is most productive of goods etc but also most productive of health and happiness. Treating people as humans, not donkeys – as equal citizens, not slaves – is best for all.

UNEMPLOYMENT AND UNDEREMPLOYMENT

There are said to be about a million Australians needing help due to their lack of adequate wage-type income. Meanwhile, government statistics say that unemployment is about 3%, and that businesses cannot get enough workers. But who can be confident of any quoted statistics now since (was it Howard's government?) it was decreed that just one hour's paid work each week meant a worker was counted as 'employed'? Maybe it's one of the faults of the RBA board members, and many policy-makers and politicians, that they never get beyond their offices (and favourite restaurants) onto the streets to visit businesses and Centrelink to find out what is true, rather than believing the rubbery figures that the desk-jockeys are reporting. Likewise we hear economists say that wages have risen by such-and-such an amount, but they should be asking *whose* wages. Politicians and pundits shouldn't be making comments about how the cost of living is affecting people without specifying which cohort they are talking about. The cost of living affects high, middle, and low-income people very differently.

ENERGY PRICES

Speaking of cost of living pressure, our electricity prices and 'natural-gas' prices have been going up completely without justification. Why has the Australian Energy Market Operator (AEMO) been allowing the energy retailers to practice their own bit of price gouging, or doesn't anyone really control the energy market? The prices of electricity have been rising at the same time cheaper renewable energy is taking over from fossil fuels – why? Again 'the market' is shown to be failing because the largely privatised energy market is wide open for gouging by the price-setters. Is this just to make the ALP government look weak and timid? Remember again that the leader of the Liberal Party, Peter Dutton, clearly stated after losing to Labor in 2022, *Our job is to make life difficult for the Albanese government.* The business sector, fossil fuel corporations, Murdoch's media, energy retailers, and (or at least so it seems) AEMO and the RBA have all been obeying this directive.

This attitude from the L/NP and influential game-players is evidently aimed at winning the game of politics rather than doing good work for the country. This childish and destructive behaviour is despite the warnings from relatively conservative identities that global heating is real and needs to be treated seriously, like adults. One such is Dr Andrew Forest, who is very keen to decarbonise industry. Another who sort-of gets the problem of global heating is Ross Garnaut whose 2019 book, *Superpower: Australia's Low-Carbon Opportunity* argued that Australia could be a great renewable energy supplier to our region.

Rapid electrification from renewable sources is the best course open to us if we want lower energy prices quickly, and to slow global heating as soon as possible. Founder of Rewiring Australia, **Dr Saul Griffith**, is an inspiring inventor, scientist, engineer and entrepreneur working in renewable energy technologies and pushing to electrify Australia. He is the author of *Electrify* (2021) and *The Big Switch* (2022). Dr Griffith is keen to see all homes, appliances and transport switched to electric technology and using renewable (sun-derived) energy. We should be supporting and publicising these efforts, yet the mainstream media rarely mentions this great work. The current federal minister, Chris Bowen, seems to be the most genuine renewables supporter in the ALP government, but he gets criticism from diverse quarters while his federal colleagues continue allowing new fossil fuel projects – totally opposite to what our survival requires.

Meanwhile the L/NP have launched an anti-renewables campaign, which, despite being a pack of lies, many people are supporting. Added to that, the mainstream media publicise this campaign regularly and rarely fact-check the Coalition's lies about a future nationally-owned nuclear power industry. I'll say more about this later, but the L/NP and their propaganda wing, News Corp, are only serving the interests of the fossil fuel corporations.

The ALP government seems to be a victim of corporate capture by the fossil fuel lobby (and by the military weapons lobby), and its efforts to rein-in the rent-seekers and far-right saboteurs has been pusillanimous, at best. For example, Origin Energy, Australia's biggest energy (gas) retailer, doubled its earnings to $1.995 billion in the first half of the financial year 2023-2024, gouging customers with ever higher bills. Logic suggests we need to get rid of the AEMO and replace the private market system with a non-market public service and a prices-justification system that serves its customers, not the profiteers. This is also why we need the promised 'National (Energy Transition) Net Zero Authority' to coordinate Australia's urgent transition to all-electric and all-renewables. It should be added that an energy system with 100% renewables, with a mix of home and EV-to-grid batteries, and some off-grid private, farm-based, or community/suburb systems, would create a much more level 'playing-field' where energy and resource access are more egalitarian and less unequal.

GROSS INEQUALITY

Australia is now profoundly unequal. An Oxfam report of 15th January 2024 stated that the combined wealth of the three richest Australians has more than doubled since 2020 at a staggering rate of $1.5 million *an hour*, while 3.25 million Australians live in poverty. Salaries have been increasing at percentage rates which compound inequalities. Now executives and professionals expect to be paid many times what ordinary workers are paid. In April 2023, while defending two ex-US Navy contractors being paid $7,500 a day by Australia, Christopher Pyne claimed that a Sydney barrister gets $5,000 a day. Meanwhile, for a single person the Jobseeker payment is $49.50 a day and a partnered person gets just $45 a day. There are many people getting huge wages while many more are unable to feed and house their families. Surely this situation must be called 'un-Australian' if anything can be. As mentioned above, Australia's 'average' salary by one measure is $94,000, yet the salary most folks earn (the *mode* wage which is **not** measured by the ABS) would be closer to half that, at around $47,000. The RBA governor gets about a million dollars a year, and the CEO of CSL received $58 million in 2022. No one can add that much value to their company, their community, or to the world. They simply can't.

To cut another long (undeserved wealth) story short, Ms Rinehart, whose father, Lang Hancock, confirmed that The Pilbara was mostly iron ore and thought 'I'll have that', is now in possession of assets worth in excess of $37 billion (according to the *Financial Review* Rich List in May 2023). How is that justified? This sort of mega-rich excessive remuneration is bad for democracy. Such super-capitalism is totally antithetical to fair democracy. One reason why is because oligarchs can and do throw their wealth and power behind corrupt regimes, the same regimes that ensure business-as-usual for those oligarchs. (Musk backed Trump and as of November 2024 will share the top job in the US 'Department Of Government Efficiency' tasked to disempower many US government institutions.)

On inequality a 2024 report from ACOSS said:

> *People in the highest 20% of the wealth scale hold nearly two thirds of Australia's wealth (64%), while those in the lowest 60% hold less than a fifth of all wealth (17%). The average income of the highest 5% income group is nearly* **nine** *times that of the lowest 20% income group; while the average income of the highest 1% income group is almost three times that of even the highest 20% income group.*
>
> https://povertyandinequality.acoss.org.au/inequality/

A study by the Australia Institute showed that the wealth of the richest 200 Australians grew from $40.6 billion to $625 billion over the twenty years from 2004 to 2014, and that wasn't all due to inflation! The wealth of those 200 people equals nearly a quarter (23.7% of GDP) of Australia's whole economy. In such an unequal society you can't talk about aggregate demand or average wage rises, you have to ask *whose* demand and *whose* wage rise. The fault with many orthodox economists is that they limit themselves to calculating macro numbers at the expense of contemplating micro realities.

As I explained in my submission to the RBA enquiry, tax cuts for the rich are inflationary – wage rises for the poor are not. It's the rich who create demand-pull inflation. Few workers are price-setters. The Laffer Curve theorem points out that zero taxation of income leads to zero revenue, but 100% income tax would also result in zero revenue because no one would have any income left, but in between those two extremes there is an ideal level of taxation where revenue is maximized. (Arthur Laffer was right, but Keynes pre-figured the idea.) This shows that tax cuts for the rich reduce tax revenue below that ideal level. Tax cuts for the rich, as demanded by Neoliberal economics and legislated in Australia by the L/NP regime, only move the revenue-take too far down the Laffer curve so that governments are not recycling our money enough for the greater good.

Far-Right politicians try to excuse tax cuts for the rich by saying, *We like to give people more of the money they earn.* Well that would be fair for many workers whose wages are so low they have to work three insecure jobs and still can't pay all their bills. Allowing every low-income earner to keep all that they earn is fair enough. A lot of working people earn so little that they should be paying little or no tax (as mentioned, a tax-free threshold at the salary that the highest number of people get would be fair and reduce churn in the system). People like the CEO of CSL cannot possibly *earn* what they bank. Neither can the RBA governor *earn* nearly a million dollars a year for wrecking home-buyers' finances. And neither did the careless boss of Robodebt *earn* hundreds of thousands overseeing the illegal scam that drove so many victims to suicide. Unjust inequality has gone far too far in Australia. This is again why:

a we need a Prices and Salaries Justification Authority, to guide maximum wages, not just the minimum wage, and
b we must reap larger taxes *from* the rich.

There's a way to restore fairness in a kind way. Because percentage wage-rises increase inequality and unfairness, flat wage rises, along with percentage wage **de**creases will restore fairness. Done well the extreme gap between the underpaid and the grossly overpaid can be reduced. Once everyone's salaries have been made reasonable, we won't have any mega-rich people to tax heavily. When that occurs, a flatter, though still progressive, income tax system would be fair. There are people who want to move away from depending on income tax, which is still the fairest tax, but doing that means having the courage to tax corporations (especially climate-destroying fossil-fuel corporations) a great deal more. Again, it's about retrieving the public's wealth/money from where it may go to languish in bank accounts or be uselessly spent on super-yachts, private jets, or billionaire's fantasies of space tourism and/or impossible colonies on the Moon or Mars. We need a different approach to economics – a circulating rather than accumulating model, an economics of enough, but never too much. That, and fairness, correcting the relentless maths of inequality, are what liberation economics is about – if it can be put into one sentence.

Apart from the maths of inequality that the more you have, the more you *can* have, and the fact that it's cheaper to live if you're wealthy, our obsession with percentages also magnifies inequality exponentially over time. For example, when a worker on an annual wage of $50,000 gets a 5% pay rise, they get an extra $2,500. But when a fortunate person on a $100,000 annual salary gets a 5% pay rise, they get $5,000 extra – twice as much. Advantage compounds advantage, and percentage rises make inequality exponentially worse. Flat increases would be fair, but percentage wage *cuts* are needed to restore fairness.

Many economists speak of average wages and other data that assumes Australia is the homogenous, egalitarian, social-democracy that it once aspired to be. But that's very far from the case now. Now the gross inequality caused by Neoliberal economics has reached the stage of creating a new pseudo-aristocracy of out-of-touch, over-privileged, rich people. The CEO-class is part of that. As above, when the RBA talks about wage rises worsening inflation we should all ask *whose* wage rises? Especially because wage rises almost never predate price rises. Higher incomes for the rich do increase inflation by adding to the demand-pull prices rises. But better incomes for minimum wage-earners and the unemployed do not increase inflation; they only reduce the poverty that causes people to go hungry, cold, homeless, un-medicated, and desperate. Higher incomes for low income earners only reduces their poor health, drug abuse, and the crime and violence caused by the desperation of poverty. The fact is that in Australia one marker of privilege is if you *can* get a salary rise – especially one that exceeds the inflation rate. Witness what a battle it is for unions to get wage increases granted for their members.

Sociologists know that the more equal a society is the better it is for everyone. As said elsewhere, there's a massively negative health cost to having an unequal society. See the 2015 book, *The Health Gap* by Professor Sir Michael Marmot. The Nordic countries score well on measures of Gross National Happiness and educational achievement not just because of their social-democratic politico-economic policies but because their citizens perceive themselves to be relatively equal. See *Viking Economics* (2016) by George Lakey. Also see the 2009 book, *The Spirit Level* by Richard Wilkinson and Kate Pickett. A recent study by the Australia Institute showed that from 2009 to 2019, 93% of the benefits of economic growth went to the richest 10%, while the bottom 90% got just 7% of the benefits.

POVERTY

As should-have-been-British-PM Jeremy Corbyn said, we should judge our economy not by the presence of billionaires but by the absence of poverty. The Australian government can and should cure poverty within a very short time. The first thing to do is to double the Jobseeker rate again. If it was doubled it would still only get back up to the poverty line. The L/NP doubled Jobseeker to soften Covid related job-losses for their middle class voters in 2020. Suddenly, as a side effect, the poorest people in Australia were able to buy essentials and pay their bills. The extra money circulating was not inflationary until Covid supply constraints gave price-setters cost-push reasons to raise prices, and later Russia's invasion of Ukraine gave an excuse to raise them more. It's only when extra money reaches the big spenders that demand-pull inflation sets in. To say that raising the Jobseeker payment is inflationary is nothing but a classist-fascist lie. The rate was doubled for Covid and it must be doubled once again.

Guardian Australia reported that many Australians are suffering financial insecurity. Dr Cassandra Goldie, the CEO of the Australian Council of Social Service (ACOSS) said, *There's no question that we've got far too many people now who just cannot make ends meet, at any time of the year.* A survey by ACOSS of Australians receiving some sort of government income support found nearly two-thirds of respondents were skipping meals or eating less to make ends meet, and more than 90% of renters were in housing stress.

As mentioned several times, the Federal government prints our currency and, within real-world capacity constraints, it can pay for whatever it chooses. It can make sure that all support payments are adequate and thereby cure poverty almost overnight. If the Federal government wants to 'balance the books' of the budget they could radically cut waste on such things as the $368 billion for AUKUS submarines (plus the $123 billion contingency fund for its inevitable cost overruns), and the (relatively minor) $500 million to rebuild the Weapons Manufacturer's Expo that used to be our National War Memorial. The federal government could afford to restore free universal public health care via a restored Medicare system, plus adding dental care to Medicare, and if that unbalanced their books, they could tax the excessively wealthy and get rid of the inefficient private health care system and health insurance industry. We've got a two-tiered health system, one level of service for the rich and a lower level for the less privileged, but it doesn't have to be that way.

The federal government could fund universal free education from early-learning child care centres all the way to university degrees, and if that unbalanced their books a bit they could increase taxes on Australia's 83% of foreign-owned mining companies that are currently repatriating Australia's mineral wealth. (And if the miners mount a scare campaign, as they did over PM Kevin Rudd's Resource Super Profits Tax in 2010, then the government just needs the courage to tell the miners to either share their profits with the country or leave the resources in the ground. Hopefully there would be no Right-wing Gillard to cave in to the capitalists.) Student debts and big-business profit-driven universities should be seen as mistakes of the past. There is no excuse for poverty in Australia in 2024. Our per-capita productivity is high (although the capitalists keep demanding that it must increase), so the job of the government is to reduce waste and fairly redistribute the nation's ample wealth.

Speaking of **productivity**, the business sector is always demanding more output for the same or less input, but logically this must tend to a limit. A farm can only produce what food it can, no matter how well you fertilize it. And a factory can only produce so many cars, no matter how you automate it and replace people with robots. Growth-mad economists see population, participation, and productivity as their key drivers of GDP growth, but there are upper limits to what each of these elements can produce, so the growthists need to stop giving free rein to their greed and start thinking about what production is truly sustainable.

Australia's minimum wage also causes poverty. While the ALP has encouraged rises in the minimum wage, those rises are still below cost of living increases, and the Australian Business Council is arguing against any rise that would allow minimum wage earners to stop going financially backwards. Cruel! Adding to the above, it is well known that poverty leads to considerably worse health outcomes – which, of course, add expense to the public health system. The 'social gradient of health' is the fact that the poorer, the less socially powerful, and the less autonomous a person is, the worse their health outcomes are, and the shorter their life expectancy. Again, see *The Health Gap* by Sir Michael Marmot.

NATIONAL DEBT

A lot of people worry about Australia's national debt, and the ALP government is using the "L/NP trillion dollar debt" as its reason/excuse for budget austerity, for not fixing housing, for not raising Jobseeker, for not curing poverty, and for not doing lots of other things that voters were hoping for from a socially responsible government. However, all these excuses are based on a misunderstanding. As stated, the sovereign (currency-creating) government of Australia does not need to have a national debt at all, and it probably should be abolished because it is just another way in which public funds are being fed to wealthy financiers rather than to social needs. The truth is the Australian government *does* have its own money tree. It's just that its fruit should be picked for need, not greed.

The national debt is controlled by the Australian Office of Financial Management at Treasury, and it issues debt instruments in the form of bonds and Treasury bills (IOUs). The various financial instruments the government uses to swap these IOUs for 'cash' (numbers on computer-held accounts) are called Australian Government Securities – AGSs. These are held by financial institutions and in the portfolios of wealthy individuals. The total of all the debts that the government has used to 'borrow money', the so-called National Debt, is a public liability but also a private asset. Again, a government that creates its own currency doesn't need to issue debt at all, so the so-called National Debt is actually a fraud upon the public.

The government securities seem mainly to be issued for the benefit of the finance sector and the rich people involved in it. The biggest problem with having a big national debt is paying the interest on the debt to all the bond/AGS holders and trying to fit that into a Federal Budget whose books don't add up well due to the lack of adequate tax revenue. In the view of an ordinary worker, our government paying interest on its totally needless debt is just crazy. Recently the ALP Treasurer, Dr Chalmers, conceded that the interest that has to be paid on the 'trillion dollar L/NP debt' is $20 billion each year. That's $20 billion that has to be 'created' and shifted to the rich and the financial sector and $20 billion that won't be going towards ending poverty or funding health, education, and the myriad other things we'd like our Federal government to fund. It has also been stated that this conduit of money going to the finance sector as interest on their 'private asset' will be at least $112 billion over the next 5 years! None of that is good for our society generally; it only benefits the bank accounts of the rich minority. This has two other effects. It increases the quantum of money in supply, and, because it is going to those who are able to spend on non-essentials, it is also highly inflationary.

There are two plausible things to do about that:

a   ignore the burgeoning money supply and keep paying the interest to the rich security-holders, whoever they may be – however this would encourage price rises, i.e. stoke inflation – or

b   make the Reserve Bank buy up all the bonds and securities, pay them out and tear them up (like they were doing during Scumo's regime).

Again, the RBA must reduce interest rates as fast as they increased them during their rate-hiking spree. Falling interest (bond-yields) should encourage bond/security holders to sell up. It will also prompt money marketeers to devalue the AUD, but perhaps it's time to take the determination of our international terms of trade out of the hands of the Forex privateers and peg our currency (and our minimum wage) against an immutable, universal, and permanent measure of value. One such measure of value would be an hour of unaided (non-mechanised) manual labour (or/and a suite of agreed goods and services), which could be used to determine exchange rates. The practice of having our bond-yield pay well just so the money markets will price our (foolishly) floating currency above junk status is bizarre. And think of all the national currencies that the money markets price as junk anyway.

At the WWII Bretton Woods conference in 1944, the international currency exchange system was pegged to gold again, but gold has a few disadvantages as a universally agreed symbol of value. Although people have desired it to roughly the same degree for millennia, people can also discount it altogether. To cut a long story short, that's what Nixon did in 1971 when the US realised they'd issued more US dollars than they had gold to guarantee it they just abandoned gold. But the world continued to use the $USD as its Reserve Currency anyway. So ever since then, the world has lived with a deliberate, structural, international inequality wherein there is little purchasing power parity (PPP) between nations, where the speculators in the money markets have ensured that the US dollar remains the world's most favoured and powerful currency, and where the US has thus-far been enabled to stay very wealthy. This unfair purchasing-power inequality has also enabled the US to keep running its 'War Economy' through its Endless War policy. Plus, the privileged position of the USD has enabled the rent-seeking of its Military Industrial Complex and lent support to its Christian nationalist, white-supremacist belief in its own exceptional 'manifest destiny' as the world's god-given superpower hegemon. Some nations in what's termed 'the global South' and in the BRICS alliance would like to change that, but it hasn't happened yet.

TAXATION

The reader may think 'tax the rich' is my only suggestion. Not so, but, starting with first principles, we need an expenditure and taxation process that circulates funds to enable our kind, fair, and equitable society. Clearly, that means *tax increases* on the very rich and on the highly profitable companies, not tax cuts. Taxes should be efficient, effective, easily administered, fair and easily complied with. They should be simple, not complicated, and not biased (i.e. not favouring the rich and powerful). Some MMT pundits claim that taxation was invented in order to create demand for a fiat currency, but this is not quite right because taxes also have a very long history and have always been imposed in order to shift wealth from those who have some (such as hard-working peasants) to those who think they can use the wealth better (such as kings and governments). Taxation was loathed even in the time of Jesus (Matthew 22:15–21 is where Jesus knew their thoughts and had them show the Roman coin – 'render unto Caesar that which is Caesar's'), so tax avoidance is not new. Taxes are really only needed to keep the currency circulating between the people and their government (just as blood must move within a body in order to do its job). This circulation is needed so enterprise and government services can operate. Taxes are also needed to control the quantity of money in circulation (i.e. the money supply) so the economy/society doesn't suffer either hypervolaemic or hypovolaemic shock (hyper-inflation or rapid deflation), but it's been many decades since governments used taxes to control the money supply and to temper demand-pull inflation. As said above, our governments must spend to provide services wherever they are needed, and tax where the money flows to (always the very rich and the big corporations) in order to keep it circulating.

What sort of taxes? Well, taxes should not be retrospective (chiefly because that's unfair), and they should only be imposed on genuinely liquid assets, like incomes and excessive savings, not on non-liquid assets like land, homes, or machinery – with maybe two exceptions:

a small annual wealth levy to shift mega-savings (e.g. Rinehart *et al*), and
  b a 'robot tax' to compensate workers for jobs lost to automation.

Taxing the big money such as corporate mega-profits is a good idea. In August 2024 The Greens called for a 'Robin Hood' tax. A global Robin Hood tax called the Tobin Tax was initially proposed by economist James Tobin in order to tax international money movements. This could provide large sums to assist in remedies for global heating. Australia's L/NP COALition has a mantra: "lower, simpler, fairer taxes", they say. Great! So don't tax the poor and workers at all – tax where the money goes – money always flows to the rich; therefore, tax the rich! Profiteering, corporations, hidden bank accounts, and stratospheric CEO incomes – tax them all – but I doubt that's what the L/NP meant by simpler and fairer taxes.

Obvious principles for good taxation include taxing what we want to discourage, like smoking and all the takings from gambling, and not taxing things we want to encourage, such as employment, as with payroll tax. As above, a small wealth tax may be needed, but, once again, only on liquid assets. It is unfair to tax people's savings, but the numbers in tax-haven bank accounts do represent some real value that could be contributing to more worthy causes.

There is also a psychological aspect to taxation, and that is that it makes people feel they are contributing to their society. When some people avoid tax (instead of being proud to contribute), they are being somewhat selfish and anti-social, so tax avoidance and tax concessions for the rich (like negative gearing and franking credits) should be abolished. As stated before, when people reach a certain level of wealth they cannot help but get richer in this system – the more you have, the more you *can* have – so it's the richest who should be most proud to return the most tax.

As an aside, there was news on 29th July 2024 that Brazil's National Secretary for Climate Change, Ana Toni, had proposed a global annual tax on the super rich to tackle the climate crisis and address poverty and inequality. Ms Toni is a member of the government of President Lula da Silva. This seems like a great idea because, to quote Forbes World's Billionaires List:

> ... *there are now* [in 2024] *more billionaires than ever: 2,781 in all, 141 more than last year and 26 more than the record set in 2021. They're richer than ever, having net worth $14.2 trillion* [USD] *in aggregate, up by $2 trillion from 2023 and $1.1 trillion above the previous record, also set in 2021.*

> https://www.forbes.com/billionaires/

The undeniable truth about neoliberal capitalism is that, despite the pandemic and several wars, the rich are getting rapidly richer while the poor are suffering more climate disasters. It need not be like that. We would all be better off with fewer oligarchs, billionaires, bankers, militarists, and mega corporations. We don't need this capitalist plutocracy; we need the biosphere to continue supporting life, and we need the mass extinction to stop. We need more egalitarian democracies where society is safe, secular, and sustainable, and where everyone has a fair quality of life. For that to happen, we need a global consensus to tax the very rich so the resources they hoard can be put to use in saving the biosphere.

Meanwhile, back in Australia we quibble about the faulty distribution of our resources. As stated, the Land tax *aka* Property tax that we pay in the form of Municipal Rates, funds the third tier of government. This tax tends to magnify postcode inequity, but since municipal councils can't issue debt-securities that a central bank will buy, they are stuck with the capital-levy, land-tax or property-tax that we call 'rates'. Any time a follower of Henry George (1839–1897) promotes the single tax called 'Land Tax' in Australia, we must all loudly remind them that *we already have one!* It's our municipal rates.

There are three types of government in Australia. First there's the Australian (Federal) Government, which can issue as much fiat currency as it likes for whatever it likes (it can also issue 'debt' to keep the money flowing to financiers). The Federal government has acquired all the big sources of revenue like income tax and the consumption tax. Secondly, there are the State governments, which can raise some debt and some taxes like stamp duties and which squabble over their share of the consumption tax (GST) that the Feds dish out. Thirdly, there are the hundreds of local governments that cannot issue debt but which rely on the one remaining source of revenue, their municipal rates as described above.

Taxation supports currency-using levels of government such as our local councils and the states, but it has a punitive and discouraging aspect too. We should tax things that are harming us and the biosphere. For example, we tax cigarettes for health reasons, but we should also tax food-miles to encourage more sustainable local food production. It is ridiculous that preserved fruit and vegetables from Europe are much less expensive on our supermarket shelves that the locally-grown Australian produce. And we should heavily tax the mining of once-only mineral deposits but then make sure all such minerals are fully recycled. The mining sector launched a huge scare campaign against Kevin Rudd's version of a 'Resource Rent Tax', threatening capital flight and job losses that were never going to happen. The Petroleum Resource Rent Tax (PRRT) is pathetically small. The Australia Institute has shown that the government takes more money from students through its CPI indexed HECS repayments than it does from all the fossil fuel corporations via the PRRT. The gas corporations profited $40 billion in 2022, but the forecast PRRT revenue will increase to only $2.7 billion in 2024–25. Data from The Australia Institute in 2023 shows that even charges on visa applications will net the government more, at $3.3 billion, and the tobacco tax will reap $13.4 billion!

Any tax on (foreign) companies extracting our mineral wealth should rightly be called the 'Resource **Depletion** Tax' and be made punitive. Maybe not quite harsh enough to stop all mining – well not yet – because we still need to build equipment and infrastructure so we can transition to a sustainable civilization. But we do need to shift to a circular economy where eventually no mining of any sort is needed. So our resource depletion taxes should be harsh enough to strongly nudge investment into 100% recycling.

The Greatly Stupid Tax (Australia's consumption tax) should be abolished because:

a   it's utterly unnecessary;
b   it is a clumsy bureaucratic burden on businesses and turns them all into tax collectors;
c   it doesn't catch black market money, as it was said to, because cash is almost exclusively used in the black economy;
d   for the growthists among us, the consumption tax *constrains* GDP; and lastly
e   the GST, *aka* the Outgo tax, is unapologetically regressive in that it hits the poorer person harder than the rich one.

The regressive nature of the GST is because every bit of an ordinary person's income is spent as outgo, and all their money is taxed coming and going. By contrast, someone with a larger income will spend a lower portion of that income on outgo and therefore the wealthy have a proportionately lower Outgo-tax burden. Admittedly, the consumption tax reaps some money from big-spending richer folks, but is that worthwhile in terms of the higher burden it imposes on poorer people, the extra costs and trouble for businesses, and the complexity of the churn of tax money going to the Federal Government and (presumably) being redistributed to the states? That's highly doubtful. Instead of the regressive GST, we should return to more progressive income taxation (as it once was) and simply tax the rich fairly.

Sadly, the states are often keen to waste whatever public money does come their way. (An example is Tasmania's government committing to spend up to a billion dollars on a stadium for the AFL Corporation when there are so many ambulances ramped at the public hospitals that none are available for emergencies.) This proposal for the abolition of the GST would leave state governments still begging for funds from the

Federal Government, which is not satisfactory for service delivery, so the federal government should return the income-taxing power to the states (from whence it came), and then the states could provide services more fairly. This would leave the Federal Government begging for a share of the states' revenue and depending on the money tree to meet Commonwealth obligations. This would cause an expanding money supply and the Federal Government applying a new tax for the purpose of controlling the quantum of money. This suggestion is in jest because it's unlikely to happen (the states are likely to be abolished first), but if the Federal Government was financially constrained, perhaps they couldn't waste public wealth on militarism or on supporting America's Military Industrial Complex as they're now doing so cheerfully.

The Federal Government has all the powers it needs in order to spend and tax for the well-being of the Australian people. We don't need a consumption tax, we just need our government to tax the incomes of the super-profitable companies digging up 'Quarry Australia' and to raise income tax on the very rich, no matter who their mates are and no matter in what tax haven they hide their money. As for blatant resource-thieves, they can be taxed at about 98% as they'd still be multi-millionaires. Alternatively, we could nationalise the whole mining sector. That has provoked coups in some countries, but it's a thought.

The Stage 3 Tax Cuts as originally legislated were fully consistent with the Neoliberal ideology of tax-cuts-for-the-rich and should've been abolished outright. They've been modified now, but the original tax cuts would have meant the almost complete abandonment of progressive taxation, and, in this deeply unequal society, that would have been extremely unfair. Oddly, Mr. Albanese says he believes in tax cuts, but we have to ask why. How is money going to circulate if taxation doesn't keep the money supply under control? There is nothing more inflationary than tax cuts for the rich. If a government relies on creating fiat money to pay for services without taxation, the end result is big numbers in rich folks' bank accounts and rapidly falling purchasing power of worker's wages, *aka* hyperinflation.

Tax cuts for the rich do not increase economic growth; they never did, even if growth was a good thing, which it isn't. Tax cuts for the rich are both highly inflationary and stupid. The ALP has a mandate for a fairer, more rational society, so, far from keeping L/NP tax cuts for the rich, the ALP government should re-impose a tax regime from a more fair and egalitarian Australia such as in the early 1950s when the top income tax rate was 75%.

https://www.abc.net.au/news/2015-04-01/tax-facts/6361050

Abolishing complicated taxes like the GST should also go along with abolishing all the very complicated and rich-people-privileging tax concessions like negative gearing. No more tax concessions to argue over; rather, one simple rule: if a person or company has pocketed more than a reasonable salary or profit, then they must repay to their society a just-proportion in the form of a progressive Income Tax (no excuses, no exceptions). And while the government is controlling demand and taxing the rich, a tax-free threshold at least as high as the minimum wage (currently $24.10 per hour, $915.90 per week or $47,626 per year) would end a lot of paperwork, reduce churn and be fairer. The simplified tax system, which operates to keep money circulating, is in harmony with the simple efficiency of recycling blood around an organic entity, and it accords with the obvious truth that the more you have the more you can have. The fair, egalitarian, efficient, and disaster-ready society will soon necessitate such radical reform becoming a priority.

By 'disaster-ready', I'm referring to the increasing climate disasters we will be facing (due to global heating) that will force us to turn all our resources to rescue, recovery, resilience, and restoration. It is for this reason that our present inefficient, time-wasting, misdirected efforts are going to have to refocus very quickly – and also refocus in the direction of world peace and cooperation. If each nation, and the world in general, fails to do this, then the mass casualties and destruction in coming decades will be SO much worse. But more on this later.

Given that the Federal Government should be controlling the money supply (quantity and price), then a serious tax reform with the aim of fairness and efficiency would cancel virtually all taxes other than a strictly regulated and progressive income-tax – along with a higher tax-free threshold as described above. Following that, the Federal Government would distribute the funds strictly according to need. This would work well with a Universal Basic Income because it would eliminate vast amounts of complexity and churn in our tax and payments systems, and it would see people paying for the goods and services that they need and want rather than seeing big money committed to the *doomed* AUKUS nuclear submarines, F-35 fighter planes, tanks, missiles and wars that almost nobody wants. A proposal such as this would require a greater level of democracy in which people would also regularly vote for where all public funds were allocated. This would see people voting for funds to go to health, education, and the whole spectrum of public services instead of to the Socialism for the Military that we see so sickeningly now.

WAR-MAKING AND A WAR ECONOMY

I'll mention the war-economy later, but when I say AUKUS is doomed, it's for two main reasons. Firstly because global heating is most likely to be hitting the world very hard before the submarines can be put into service, and secondly because the US seems doomed. Plus, Australia joining America's nuclear-armed Triad with US or UK built submarines (which will almost certainly carry nuclear weapons secretly) is insane, both economically and strategically. Love of war-making is a sickness.

Next, America is a sick society. It's so sick with gun-love that it's almost a war zone. In the year up to the 7th December 2023, there were 632 mass shootings in the US, 647 in 2022, and 690 in 2021. Tens of thousands of people are needlessly killed or wounded by guns each year in the US. And more importantly, the US is so bitterly divided politically that Trump's victory in the 2024 Presidential elections could easily result in a new Civil War breaking out. The only issue that unites the right-wing Democrats and the crazy, far-Right Republicans is their confected rivalry with China. Just as the US was in bitter rivalry with the USSR, so too the bitterly divided US is unified behind the American military's 'containment' policy against China. Paranoia and xenophobia have bred a new external 'enemy' to justify more military spending, unify the majority of the people, and distract them from their economic woes. The US is so divided that it will soon be the dis-united states. Despite their professed Christianity, it seems few have read Luke 6:27 – 'love your enemies', John 13:34 – 'love one another', and/or Matthew 12:25 – 'a nation divided against itself will not survive'.

Speaking of 'values', as an aside, I'd argue that 'the West's' current democracies are not so great if we get (pathological) liars like Morrison, Johnson and Trump in charge of the AUKUS countries. We should look at the values we share with other cultures rather than the oft-repeated and supposed 'different' values we are supposed not to share with communist China. I'm talking about basic aims like wanting a safe and happy future for our children, or wanting peace and security for those we love and for all our descendents. Finding points of agreement rather than rushing to enmity seems wise. Both Australia and the US should try more diplomacy rather than militarism as the path to solving international tensions. Of course, we don't want to live under any lying dictator or new tsar, but many argue China isn't as undemocratic as it's portrayed by the western media and is mostly made paranoid over security due to the constant meddling by the US military, the CIA *et al*.

Just as China needs to make itself attractive to the Taiwanese so that reunification can be peaceful, so too must the West make much better forms of democracy if the idea of government by the people is going to reap the rewards of universal health and happiness that an equal and empowered populace could enable. Our democracies have not fulfilled that happy promise because of neoliberal capitalism and because there have not been adequate institutions to filter out the corrupt people and those with malignant intentions. In fact, corporate consumer capitalism has often encouraged malignant leaders. That's why we've been afflicted with rubbish regimes like those of 'Scumo', 'Bozo', and 'the orange-painted idiot' who has been re-elected POTUS in November 2024.

The re-election of Trump shows that at least 72 million Americans are actively in favour of a sneering, lying, convicted criminal who was indirectly responsible for hundreds of thousands of deaths through a stupid response to the Covid-19 pandemic; the man whose bruised ego made him deny his 2020 loss and incite the violent attempted coup on 6th January 2021; a known 'white supremacist'; a racist, misogynist, narcissistic, science-illiterate, climate-denying, neo-Fascist, wanna-be dictator. Trumps followers have won enough seats in the US Congress to ensure his dictatorship. His supporters have vowed to implement the far-Right Project 2025, and now this person is set to take charge of the dying US hegemony. Despite not being threatened by any country the US still has the world's biggest military arsenal and Trump is going to be its commander in chief – again. Is this the man and the country that Australia *really* wants to have as our number one ally?

At the time of writing the US is enabling Israel to make a hideous war in western Asia, chiefly an attempted genocide of Palestinians, an annihilation of the Lebanese response to that genocide, and a shadow war against Iran. Having trashed Gaza and made it uninhabitable for its 2.2+ million people, the Zionists have started on a similarly murderous program against all their other neighbours. The US is also supporting war in Ukraine against Russia and they are grooming Australia, the Philippines, Japan and South Korea to make war on China, with Taiwan as the excuse. The US is at its most dangerous because its hegemony is failing. There never was a moral foundation to US militarism, but neoliberal greed capitalism has succeeded in making more and richer billionaires instead of giving its people and US society a raison d'être. The people are nihilistic because project hegemony is no longer enough for them. As they see themselves losing global dominance their chronic paranoia becomes much worse. The US is failing so badly that they are hurting themselves and doing stupid things like banning imports of Chinese electric vehicles.

Australia should cut free of the US, especially the American military, which has groomed successive Australian governments and which continues to walk all over Australia's sovereignty. Australia has followed the US military into repeated war-failures – Korea, Vietnam, Afghanistan, and Iraq to name the most obvious. We've sunk billions into hopeless US military equipment such as the F-35 Strike Fighter and allowed the increasing interoperability of Australian and US armed forces, unimpeded US use of Australian bases, B-52 bombers carrying nuclear weapons to operate out of Australian air bases, submarines in WA, and Pine Gap (in NT) and other installations to assist US military operations and intelligence gathering. Our government even encourages US military and intelligence personnel to be embedded within Australia's intelligence and defence organisations.

As mentioned earlier, the federal ALP government has been gulled into paying $4.59 billion AUD ($3 billion USD) to the US submarine building industry for no more than a promise to sell us some second-hand submarines sometime in the coming decades. The planned AUKUS program has been guesstimated to cost $368 billion AUD; that's over $33 million every day for the next 30 years! (Think of all the hospitals, homes, and services that $33 million per day could fund.) And as of 17th April 2024, Minister Richard Marles wants to spend $16–21,000,000,000 for Australia to have missiles that should never be used and to increase our military spending to 2.4% of GDP – all to please American warmongers. Given this, how can any Federal Government say they can't find money for health, housing, education, or care for our vulnerable? And how can any government pretend they need to chase tiny 'tax debts' or persecute the poor for mythical welfare overpayments?

The term **'war economy'** describes what many countries (and particularly the US) have noticed and that is there's a war-time boom in the economy and the boom often extends for some time post-war. The military-industrial-complex that President Eisenhower warned of in his farewell address in 1961 has taken over the government of the US and melded with the fossil fuel corporations to enact a doctrine of perpetual war in US policy, by which public money is circulated very generously through that military-industrial-fossil-fuel sector. This war economy has served the US well since WWII, but it has served the rest of the world tragically. While the US has seen itself as the world's policeman, it has tended to shun the opinions of the majority world, as voiced through the United Nations, and starved that organisation of the resources needed to do its job properly. My point is that Australia should not be trying to mimic the US war economy or continue our present integration into the now-global military-industrial-fossil-fuel complex. Some interesting reading is the 2008 book, *The Complex: How the Military Invades Our Everyday Lives*, by Nick Turse.

Sam Wainwright of Australia's Socialist Alliance was correct when he wrote that the US is hell-bent on blocking China both economically and militarily. One would have to say that such action is extremely unfair and hypocritical, but the confected jealousy of China is one of the few things that has consensus in American political circles. The singular issue that unites Americans is the crazy idea of 'the containing of China'. Now that Trump has won the 2024 US presidential election there's no doubt his regime will continue this aggression towards Australia's most significant trading partner.

The US and Australian governments, plus the Right-wing media, constantly exaggerate Chinese aggression, but China's response is essentially defensive. China is the country being encircled by US military bases, alliances, and missile systems, not the US. Shared military adventures and projects of the Christian-imperialist military establishment, led by the US – such as invasions, wars, AUKUS, and the Five Eyes spy group – not only arise from a delusion of shared culture but also from shared economic interests. The US and UK are the biggest foreign investors in Australia and the biggest recipients of overseas investment by Australians. But there's a big irony in Australia joining the aggressive American push to 'contain' China because not only is China Australia's biggest trading partner, but it is also a much nearer neighbour in our region. The US and UK share the opposite side of the planet. The Australian government wants to have its cake and eat it too – to join the US, UK, and others in blocking China while also retaining all the benefits of trade with China.

Australia's current Defence Policy explained satirically in an episode of *Utopia*:

> https://www.youtube.com/watch?v=sgspkxfkS4k

This two-faced pro-militarist approach is not sustainable in the face of global heating and against the reality that the US is in all sorts of decline. It doesn't have to be this way. Australia needs to be independent, neutral, and peace-loving. We cannot always be looking toward one set of bully-boy nations to protect us from the supposed threat of other bully-boy nations. We should achieve our peace with multilateral ties to the region we are in. We need to accept that we are geographically and demographically a South-East Asian nation. As Paul Keating put it, we need to find our security *within* Asia, not *from* Asia. Getting sucked into the pointless rivalry from the US against China, and increasing the possibility of nuclear war in our region, is madness, but that's what Australia's 'defence' department is doing.

WAR BEGETS WAR

Always, violence begets violence, militarism begets militarism, and war begets war. This is an axiom we should remind ourselves of every day. Its converse should be true too, that peace begets peace. Given that damage from more unstable climates are already causing major problems (and will only get rapidly worse), we urgently need to establish a global culture of live-and-let-live, peaceful coexistence and world peace in order to unite in combating global heating. So it's stark raving insane that Australia has been roped into America's Nuclear Triad via the AUKUS subs, B-52s and US bases.

Promoting the Land Forces war-making Expo in Melbourne on September 11th 2024, on ABC RN, Bec Shrimpton, a Director at the Australian Strategic Policy Institute, (ASPI is part funded by the US State Department) said of the anti-war protesters:

> *I understand that people have a right to express their opinion, and of course understand the instinct for the anti-war protests, but unfortunately the world is not as we would all like it to be and is not a peaceful and stable place at the moment.*

And she went on to defend the military expo. This event, which hoped to draw over 1,000 military-related corporations from 31 countries, was mounted at a time when the horrors inflicted by Netanyahu's Zionists on the civilians of Israel's concentration camp (called Gaza), and the Zionists' attempted genocide of the Palestinian people had been live-streamed to us for eleven months. And it came just one day after the Israelis had used an 'earthquake bomb' on what they'd told displaced Palestinian families – who were living in tents – was a safe zone. The crater that was left after the tent-dwellers were vapourised would have held a three storey house!

As if holding a pro-war exposition for the international Military Industrial Complex (MIC) was not bad enough, to do so at this time was an absolutely breathtaking insult to all humane Australians. Plus, a thousand heavily armed police were set against the 2–3,000 protesters. The police, using horses, shields, batons, and in full riot gear, were firing rubber bullets, tear gas, exploding flash-bang grenades, and spraying pepper-spray in the faces of protesters who sought to blockade the weapons expo. The police came well prepared to start a fight, so at least some of their bosses must have known what an insult the war expo was. Apart from a number of violent masked men who were suspected *agents provocateurs*, most of the protesters were non-violent peace-lovers. And to add insult to insult, the deputy leader of the federal L/NP, Sussan Ley, called the protest 'nonsense' and told Sky News ... *these people need to get a job ... it's like 'rent a crowd' every single time we see one of these protests* .... Later, Victoria's Labor Premier, Jacinta Allan, who reportedly spent $10 million on the army of police and brought in extra police from NSW, followed this insult by saying, *Any industry deserves the right to have these sorts of events in a peaceful and respectful way* – as if the most evil industry in the world was merely having a harmless trade fair.

We should ask ourselves if this is the Australia we want, a police state where militarised police attack citizens so the multinational MIC and the

US military hegemony can hold a back-slapping fair where they celebrate their latest play-things for murdering people?

Let's not forget that under the L/NP regime in 2018, when Christian Porter was AG and Peter Dutton was Minister for Home Affairs (with Mike Pezzullo), they amended the 1903 Defence Act to permit "the Prime Minister or other 'authorising' ministers to call out the military, or pre-authorise deployment." This gave the executive, including Mr Dutton, the authority to order Australian soldiers to not only act against Australian citizens – such as climate protesters blockading a coal port – but also to shoot to kill Australians, and not even questions in Parliament would be allowed. If you don't believe me, read this:

> https://www.unswlawjournal.unsw.edu.au/wp-content/uploads/2019/05/2019-5-HEAD.pdff

As said, violence begets violence, militarism begets militarism, and war begets war. I'm convinced that militarists are trapped in a culturally acquired maladaptive belief system. As Bec Shrimpton unthinkingly rolled out the usual assumption that humans will always be making war on one another, she showed just how entrenched the maladaptive disorder of **belligophilia** really is. Militarism, this insane love of war, is accelerating us on our already accelerating race to the end of civilization – and even to our extinction.

The reason for harping on about the evils of militarism is that our *economics of restoration and fairness* can hardly get started if there is still the hyperthreat of war that is destroying and killing and distracting us from addressing *the super-mega-threat of global heating*. As the extreme weather events progressively overwhelm our homes and our capacity to grow food, if human-kind doesn't learn to live and let live then we are not going to save ourselves. Please consider these overlapping events in 2023–2024:

While Australia topped the 1.5° C level in 2023, the year up to the time of writing has seen many severe weather events. In November 2023 Storm Bettina struck the Black Sea area, affecting over 2.5 million people and causing 23 deaths. In February 2024 wildfires in Chile destroyed over 14,000 homes and killed 131 people. In March–April heat-waves in North Africa and the Sahel may have killed thousands. In late April to early May Brazil's southernmost state of Rio Grande do Sul was affected by flooding, displacing 600,000 people and causing 150,000 injuries and 169 deaths. In April there were flash floods in the Persian Gulf region. From March to May flooding in East Africa affected 700,000 people and caused hundreds of deaths. In the same period Myanmar reported 1,500 deaths from heat stroke; while in Brazil flooding affected 478 cities, killed 173 people, injured 806, and displaced over 423,000 people. In May a storm in Texas killed 5 and left 600,000 without power. In the same month cyclonic storm Remal killed at least 84 people in India and Bangladesh. In May–June Mexico had extreme heat and at least 125 people died from heat-related illnesses. In June at least 1,170 pilgrims died in Saudi Arabia in an intense heat wave with temperatures reaching over 50° C during the Hajj. Also in June heavy rain in Bangladesh caused landslides and floods that left nearly 2 million people stranded. Meanwhile wildfires burned about 440,000 hectares in the Brazilian Pantanal wetlands. In July hurricane Beryl was a strong Atlantic hurricane that affected parts of the Caribbean, United States, and Yucatán Peninsula. It killed 64 people and caused more than US $5 billion in damages. Also in July a deadly heat-wave in the Mediterranean resulted in at least 23 fatalities. There were wildfires in the Amazon, Africa and Canada. The Canada wildfires seemed to be an extension of the unprecedented 2023 wildfires. The unusually long 2023 fire season continued into the autumn and the fires smouldered through the winter. About 150 fires re-ignited in February. By May, large wildfires were burning in British Columbia, Alberta, and Manitoba. Later there were fires in The Northwest Territories, Saskatchewan, Labrador and Newfoundland. There were heat waves during the Summer Olympics. A heat wave in Greece killed a number of people including Dr Michael Mosley in June. During that northern summer Mexico reported over 100 heat-related deaths and thousands of cases of heat stroke. In the northern part of India's south-western state, Kerala, an extreme monsoon downpour on 30th of July caused landslides that killed hundreds of people. PNG also had deadly landslides. September alone was a month of disasters. On the 3rd of September, after a week of destructive storms over South Eastern Australia, it was reported that, on average, August 2024 was Australia's hottest August on record. September continued with flooding in Uşak in Türkiye; Super Typhoon Yagi crossed eight countries in East Asia; floods occurred in Teruel, Spain; in Mecca, Saudi Arabia; Zapopan, Mexico; Jumilla, Spain and Marseille in France. By 11th of September a combination of drought, flood, and a civil war in Sudan left 25 million people at risk of starvation and the World Health Organisation said 3.6 million children are malnourished. Floods affected Nigeria and Italy later in the month. Before September was over hurricane Helene was probably the most damaging hurricane yet in the US, and although only about 247 people were killed, 40 million people were left without power and the damage caused may exceed the cost of any previous storm to hit North America. On 30th of September over 200 people were killed in floods and landslides in Nepal. A month later at the end of October a year's worth of rain fell in a few hours on the Valencia region of Spain killing nearly 300 people.

In the week prior to the Melbourne Land Forces war expo, Super Typhoon Yagi had killed hundreds. That was a tropical cyclone that started east of the Philippines in early September and progressed westward over South China and Southeast Asia, causing death and damage across eight countries. From the Philippines it affected Hong Kong, Macau, Hainan island, southern Guangxi province, Vietnam, Laos, southern Yunnan province, northern Thailand and Myanmar. Its remnants then helped form a deep depression in the Indian Ocean which brought flooding to Bangladesh and India. A series of storms affected Tasmania and Victoria between 26th August and 4th September leaving over 180,000 customers without power in the two states. A week after the September 11th Land Forces weapons expo, on the 17th of September, a storm called Boris caused the biggest floods in central Europe in decades with tens of thousands evacuated, and 250,000 homes affected. Meanwhile there were wildfires in Portugal, and Shanghai was hit with the biggest typhoon in 75 years. The mainstream media may deny the obvious signal of global heating, but it is right there, juxtaposed against the militarists' back-slapping glee over their highly profitable preparations for World War 3. Surely this is maladaptive and insane. The callous and murderous way the Israeli regime exploded communication devices in Lebanon (18th & 19th of September 2024) demonstrates the sort of dystopia that the war-makers are taking us into as they ignore the collapse of Earth's life support systems. Everything is linked to everything else. Why is there so much focus on making war yet so little is being done about the accelerating disasters from climate change? Will we choose life, or death?

If we are ever to truly break down the militarists' maladaptive belief system and stop its behaviours and policies of murdering in the most horrible way, and murdering the most people it can at any one time, then we must cure the war-love mental illness first.

WHOSE VALUES?

The dual hell-scape described above is a harbinger of where Australia's pro-American, pro-military 'leaders' want to take us. Yet these same politicians and media mouth-pieces love to cite the idea of 'shared values' across the capitalist, English-speaking world. But does that claim of shared values bear close scrutiny? Despite what many believe, most Australians do not share American values, quite the opposite. Australia is a more science-respecting, peace-loving, multicultural, majority-secular nation. Australia does have a diverse and sometimes vocal minority who still hold to an imaginary deity. We have many religious groups and at the 2021 census 39% of us said we are free of religion. That number is increasing. By contrast, only 28% are free of religion in the US, and in 2021 a majority 63% of Americans claimed to be Christians. Americans tend to cling more to superstitions and traditions than Australians. The United States is so fanatically Judeo-Christian that many American Christians actively support Zionism, and their religious bigotry is nearly as misogynist as the Afghan Taliban, with abortion and other women's rights being made illegal in many states. Many American communities are imposing Judeo-Christian mythology in schools, canonical books are being banned, and proven science such as evolution and climate science are being denied. Many Americans want to deny their history of slavery.

Australians like to think we are egalitarian and community-minded and that we'll look out for each other and care for our mates, even though that's less true than it was. By contrast, the US is one of the most unequal societies and has worse poverty than Australia. Americans insist on individual freedom and the idea that if you're poor it's your own fault and your problem to cope with – without help. Many in the US have lost a sense of purpose since many worthwhile jobs were transferred to low-wage countries. Nihilism set in deeply as the rust-belts and inequity widened, and many Americans turned to narcissist-Trump, who blames everyone and everything other than the real problem, namely, neoliberal capitalism. It's as if Australians had made Pauline Hanson our Prime Minister. You would have thought that Trump's habitual angry sneer, strongly suggesting an antisocial personality disorder, would have warned American voters not make him President again, but it's happened.

Here's a vital point that needs repeating: what the two ignorant, xenophobic 'conservatives' American Trump and Australian Hanson have in common is that they both blame minorities (and people they claim are different races) for economic problems caused by the exact same ultra-capitalism they unthinkingly champion. They claim loudly that they have all the answers to every problem when in truth they have nothing good or original to offer society. Sadly, many people follow their angry rhetoric. It must be recalled that economic problems set the stage for the rise of the Nazis, and many people were inspired by the angry rhetoric of the demagogue who led them to start WWII. Keeping nasty fascists out of power is partly a moral and cultural problem, but primarily it is an economic problem.

Australians mostly prefer to live and let live. We're mostly tolerant of difference and diversity, we don't ban books, and we don't try to tell women what to do with their bodies. Australians are also fortunate enough to have obligatory and preferential voting, so we elect our politicians more directly and democratically, and all sections of society are included (Our politicians are not yet as representative as they should be, but that and the level of diversity is slowly growing.) In contrast, parts of the US electoral system are actively engaged in voter suppression (Google it) to exclude sections of society such as African-Americans and Hispanics. In further contrast, most Australians would be comfortable living in a peaceful, pluralist, multipolar world with multilateral international relations. Unlike America, we are not wedded to the idea of national exceptionalism, and we haven't got a global military hegemony to maintain. Our head of state is a useless figure-head in another country, not the chief of our military. Americans are the most war-loving nation in history (Jimmy Carter said so). From 1965 to 1975, the United States dropped more than 7.5 million tons of bombs on Vietnam, Laos, and Cambodia – twice the tonnage bombed during the whole of World War II. US wars have left horrid legacies in many countries. Was the Vietnam war conducted for fear of a slightly different political-economy called Communism, or was it because the Military Industrial Complex wanted to keep public money flowing to its owners? Americans imagine the world will forgive and forget all that they've done in so many other countries, but are we Australians wise to do so?

Unfortunately, trends toward Americanization in Australia have been strong for a long time. Partly due to the American Murdoch's media dominance that broadcasts Right-wing disinformation, partly due to all the US entertainment we get, and partly due to our American neoliberal economics, our supposed culture of fairness and kindness has been Americanised into a more aggressive, competitive, anti-intellectual, shallow, showy, selfish individualism. Australia always had a lot of racism, but the US is more torn by the racist legacy of slavery. The myth of 'white supremacy' is still strong in the US. Sadly, partly due to globalization and partly due to Right-wing 'culture wars', we are trending toward more racism, misogyny, and toxic ultra-nationalism. I feel that due to News Corp *et al*, our social cohesion is fraying. Americanisation has led to our government adopting all the US foreign policy stances without question, and Australia's government wants to build an arms industry in imitation of America's socialism-for-the-military style of war-economy. The executive of the federal ALP appears to want to support the US in making war on China. Given the history of those two countries, we should be much more afraid of the US than of China.

This may surprise you, but hear me out. I consider it much more likely that the US will attack Australia than China or any other country. The Americans alone have important bases and soldiers here. They are flying heavy bombers out of the northern territory and they have almost complete control of Australia's military. The ALP government is not just afraid of a coup if they question US activities, as happened to Gough Whitlam, but I think they are quietly afraid that if we so much as asked them to leave us alone then the US would bomb our cities with the same sort of careless glee with which the Israeli army is bombing homes and shooting children throughout Gaza and Lebanon. Who are the real enemies of peace?

Australia needs to be neutral. I admit I support the Independent and Peaceful Australia Network (IPAN), but look at our geography on the globe – we are much better off staying out of other people's wars. People will roll out the usual old sayings like, "if you want peace then prepare for war" or "you've got to show strength to deter an enemy", but global heating means we have to be way past that nonsense now. We cannot afford for the boys to play their war games at murdering others and stealing land. The first thing for Australia to do is get a security pact with the American regime to get them to promise not to attack us. It won't be worth much more than the paper it's written on, but even getting such a symbolic treaty from the most war-loving nation in history will be an achievement. Second, but at the same time getting a security pact with China to ensure continued peaceful trade and cooperation would be great. We could just let all the military hardware rust away to dust. Our whole species urgently needs peace and cooperation like never before in our history.

SOCIALISM FOR THE MILITARY

This term describes the fact that the military sector is given preferential treatment in almost every country in the world. Military personnel get social housing and good pensions for themselves and their families. Such benefits are fair and necessary. After all, soldiers get trained to be murderers and may be murdered or injured (mentally or physically) in any of the idiotic wars they get sent to – and they and their families have to contend with the awful results. It's just that military-captured governments give social benefits and respect to the military that should be available to everyone.

Then there are the war toys. The military can get almost all the super-expensive, highly polluting equipment they ask for, while governments impose cruel austerity on all other parts of society. The most socialist aspect of militarism is all the public funds (real wealth) that gets funneled to the Military-Industrial-Security Complex that has colonised most countries. Departments of defence should be called Departments of Militarism, or departments of support for the rent-seeking military weapons companies. War-making gets all it asks for, while the peace-making United Nations is starved of funds and deliberately weakened, abused by the fascist-minded, and ignored. This is clearly a social and economic problem because, as our resources dwindle as a result of increasing climate-related disasters, we'll have fewer resources to rectify global heating. And those resources are not being – and will not be unless there's radical change – allocated in a rational or kindly manner. To allocate so many human and material resources to murderous and destructive war-making rather than to agriculture, shelter, and restoring the biosphere, is insane. I would argue that all our military personnel and resources must be re-trained and redirected for climate-emergency rescues, clean-ups, restoration, and building resilience. To reach for survival, we will need all the help we can get, which means transitioning 100% of our military to the tasks of biosphere guardianship.

Clearly, then, it's totally against Australia's interests to get involved in the arrogant project of the incompetent American hegemony to 'contain' China. The propagandists cite the Chinese military build-up but fail to explain why China has *been forced* to muscle-up its military. People forget that the US was provoking war with China *before* 11th of September 2001. One example was during the NATO bombing of Yugoslavia in 1999 when only one US bombing mission was organized and directed by the CIA. That was on the night of the 7th of May when five US precision-guided bombs hit the Chinese embassy in Belgrade, killing three Chinese journalists. Many believed the bombing was just to show the Chinese what the American guided weapons were capable of. Another example was the Hainan Island incident which began on the 1st of April 2001. The United States was flying a signals intelligence aircraft south-east of China's Hainan Island when it was intercepted by two Chinese interceptor jets. One of those Chinese planes collided with the US spy plane resulting in the crash death of the Chinese pilot and an emergency landing by the American plane. After ten days of negotiation, the incident was resolved diplomatically. Incidents like these no doubt focused Chinese government thinking on defence.

On 26th of May 2022 this incident was all but repeated when an Australian RAAF P-8 Poseidon A47-008 'surveillance' (spy) plane was intercepted by a Chinese J-16 fighter over the South China Sea in the region of the Paracel Islands. The Chinese pilot did what he could, short of a lethal attack, to force the spy plane away from China's 'territorial line'. Is flying spy planes near China *really* RAAF business? Why was an Australian plane so far away from Australia's territorial waters? We all know – it was among other Australian assets playing 'deputy sheriff' for the American Military.

Here's a link to a report by Professor Wanning Sun via the independent journal, Crikey. Professor Sun quotes Ross Garnaut at a symposium at the ANU in mid-August 2024. Regarding US-Australia relations, Garnaut said:

> *There is no future for our two peoples and there may be no future for humanity unless our U.S. ally can get used to being one of several powerful states in a world that allows primacy to none of them.*

> https://www.crikey.com.au/2024/08/20/china-ambassador-ross-garnaut-aukus/

In January 2024, China put sanctions on the US in protest at further US weapons going to Taiwan, but if (for analogy) China was increasing an already huge armament of (say) US territory Puerto Rico against the United States, had already imposed sanctions against the US, was doing 'freedom of navigation' naval patrols off Miami, had many military assets in the Caribbean, and was threatening the US from hundreds of surrounding bases, what would the US do? American militarism drives every other country into militarism, either as allies or rivals. But of course, any arms race boosts the profits of the arms industry.

There is no excuse for tolerating any war-making, especially not if the chief aim of the military-murder-industry is just profit. Militarism and war-making are morally unacceptable besides being highly mal-adaptive. War-making is the most anti-economic, anti-human behaviour that we humans perform. On top of being a waste of everyone's resources, and the cause of inestimable suffering, wars wouldn't happen if there was no militarism. If there was no militarism there would be no military build-ups and no arms races where nations provoke each other down the vortex into war. You would've thought we'd have learnt that lesson from the arms race that led to World War I, but here we are over 110 years later and still the arms races are accelerating. And the madness of burning too many fossil fuels is linked to these foolish military rivalries because there's the constant hunt for new oil for new wars, and new wars for oil as well. War for oil for oil for war is a spiral of insanity!

As stated earlier, I'm convinced that militarists (either in or out of uniform) are afflicted with a psychological disorder called belligophilia, or love-of-war. This is a global human problem, and it's the biggest obstacle to world peace, international security, and especially to effective climate action. As some clever person suggested, wouldn't it be a great day when hospitals and public schools were generously funded while the military had to hold lamington drives in order to buy guns, bombers, tanks and submarines. The image of macho militarists selling cakes to buy their weapons of mass-murder is so incongruous it's hilarious. It's unlikely, but I hope they are reduced to that very soon, then we'll be on the way to world peace. Such a situation would be vastly more sustainable than our present war-wracked, economy-wrecking and ecologically suicidal civilization. We not only need a sustainable economy that doesn't exceed Earth's carrying capacity, we also need to direct all our resources into restoration, so that leads us back to economics as planetary care.

STEADY-STATE ECONOMY

Most national economies have a fluctuating business cycle. They are either expanding or contracting, or somewhere in between. They can either be rising into grief with some level of inflation, or falling into grief with deflation or depression. Many economists have considered how to smooth the business cycle, and neoliberalism decided to go for endless growth as a way to do that. Of course, endless growth is impossible, so there goes that theory! But we can tend towards a steady-state and sustainable economy if governments make the effort to maintain some economic homeostasis. We can also tend towards a steady-state global economy if we have an agreed value for our currencies that is fixed to labour (this could be the basis of an Earth Standard Currency). However, if your unit of currency is permanently equal to an hour of unaided human work this means (in theory at least) the minimum wage should never rise, which could see low-wage workers feeling hopeless. The temptation would be to re-value against the labour standard so that minimum wages had more purchasing power. But this would only spark a race to the bottom, so re-valuing against the labour standard would defeat the benefits of having an internationally fixed currency. The only just way to make this work and avoid disharmony over expectations is to keep conditions reasonably egalitarian and fair. This would require governments to strictly control prices, as far as possible, and to also fix a maximum wage that is steadily brought back down to fairness. The way to do this fairly is to take advantage of the compounding effect of percentages. Wage disparity is created by percentage pay rises, but the process can work in reverse. Simply have universal flat rises in wages so the low-waged are brought up, and simultaneous percentage decreases in salaries so that (done judiciously) the high-waged are brought down to a fair wage. Plus a progressive tax on the rich, of course. The importance of pegging the value of your currency to something immutable (as I've suggested elsewhere, an hour of manual labour) is that global currencies share an approximately universal value, which would finally make international trade more-or-less fair. The two big difficulties this idea will face are firstly getting global agreement, and secondly keeping prices fair as climate damage draws down resources and devastates supplies.

Pegging your currency to the fixed value of labour will, of course, affect foreign exchange. When any nation wants to trade with another country whose currency is fixed, they will have to equate minimum wage to minimum wage, so firstly this cuts out the foreign exchange markets, secondly it means that no currency (e.g. the USD) can be privileged over another, and thirdly there would no longer be so much profit in sending industries to slave-wage countries like Bangladesh *et al*. Added to that, there would no longer be any need for a 'reserve' currency as all currencies (global South and North) would be obliged to have comparable value, fixed to the labour-standard, no matter what each country called their currency. This would also encourage national self-sufficiency because some countries might try to leverage their natural advantages and not trade fairly when they couldn't exploit others the way the global North is still (since colonial times) exploiting the global South. Instead we'd see a rather more fair and egalitarian international community.

Such an egalitarian global economy would tend to prompt co-operation and peace between countries, and it would mean much less economic power in the hands of a would-be hegemon.

Just two instances will serve to illustrate how economic power has been weaponised. For years, the US steadily imposed more sanctions and intervened economically and politically against the government of Venezuela, culminating in 2019 in what was a coup de grâce on the country causing the worst humanitarian crisis South America has seen. Also, after twenty years of war-making in Afghanistan, the US froze the assets of that country in 2021 thus compounding the disaster of their retreat and the return of the Taliban. Such abuses of economic power would be much less possible in a world where there are no currencies that are privileged over any others. But there is another implication of pegging currencies to a fixed value, and that is something called the Economic Trilemma, or Impossible Trinity.

The Trinity Theory, also known as the Monetary Trilemma, states that a country cannot have free capital movements, an independent monetary (interest rate) policy, and a fixed foreign exchange rate all at once. The theory says that these three don't work together; it has to be any two of those three. This theory is from the 1960s, but I submit that a country can have a fixed value for its currency, and therefore fixed foreign exchange rates, plus set its own interest rates, and would be self-harming to have no controls on foreign capital movements anyway. A nation that lets foreigners invest at will and expatriate the profits, without any tax paid, is betraying its people. So as I see it, the theory doesn't stand up.

IT'S THE *ECOLOGY*, STUPID!

The ecology of everything is what we must focus on, not the economy of making ever more money. To lift a definition from Wikipedia, ecology is the scientific study of:

> ... *the relationships among living organisms, including humans, and their physical environment. Ecology considers organisms at the individual, population, community, ecosystem and biosphere level.*

Our own ecology would be a good place to start. Humans need food and water. It's a very basic principle of ecology that no organism can take more from its environment than its environment can give. Any population that overpopulates or in some other way outstrips the sustainable resources of its home is destined for a collapse. We are taking more from Nature than the biosphere can give, and we are degrading its productive capacity while we are at it. I highly recommend that everybody read the 2005 book

Collapse: How Societies Choose to Fail or Succeed by Professor Jared Diamond. His considerations in *Collapse* are an examination of the meta-ecology of human societies. Professor Diamond's quiet warnings are more vital than ever. Much of our food comes from broad-acre, monocultural agriculture that's processed and trucked into our supermarkets. This is a big vulnerability, especially for city-dwellers. Subsistence farming might prove to be a little more resilient to climate disasters. Politicians and children too often think that shops are where food comes from. We also overlook that our bodies run on solar energy that's been synthesized into a huge range of useful compounds by green, photosynthesizing plants on land and plankton in the oceans. No photosynthesizing, no life. As someone said, 'As plankton goes, all life on Earth will follow'. We can only thrive in a healthy biosphere. The billionaires who dream of colonies in space just don't grasp all the vital services that Nature provides for us. They need to be reminded that there are no fish and chips with fresh Caesar salads on Mars.

And their ambitions for space travel highlight a couple of those natural services – all the associated jet travel is making global heating worse, and the rocket launches are depleting atmospheric ozone. Instead, governments and billionaires should be urgently focused on keeping life on Earth. If we don't do that there soon won't be any fish and chips with fresh Caesar salad on Earth either. The moon and Mars can take care of themselves.

Here's a 15 minute video by Dr Howard Dryden, of the GOES Foundation, at COP26. In this presentation Dr Dryden describes research from the Global Oceanic Environmental Survey (GOES) which shows that unless we stop using a range of toxic chemicals, then Earth's marine ecosystem will collapse in the next 15 to 20 years.

https://www.youtube.com/watch?v=ORGxHr7GqrQ

We not only have to plant a trillion trees & stop using Fossil Fuels, but the easiest thing we MUST do is STOP USING TOXIC CHEMICALS and keep ALL of our pollution out of the oceans! Here's a link to a vital YouTube video, **How to save the planet, part 2 with audio**:

https://www.youtube.com/watch?v=p4ffwzLCw-o

GEOENGINEERING

For many decades, climate scientists have been warning about the irredeemable end of the global heat balance – which was kept stable for millions of years by the living biosphere itself. We humans have been conducting *unconscious* geoengineering ever since we started burning the various fossil hydrocarbons in large quantities. Our aggressive destruction of forests has for many decades energized the process of turning bare ground into drought-stricken, dust-storm desert. Plus, our pollution of the oceans has made them too hot, acidic and contaminated for them to continue sequestering CO_2 and topping up our oxygen supply.

It may seem minuscule at present, but atmospheric oxygen is dropping at 4 parts per million per year. Obviously, when we burn anything oxygen gets taken from the atmosphere and tied up in CO_2. Only green & living type things reverse that reaction significantly. **We must stop burning things, anything!** When we burn fossilized hydrocarbons in our estimated two billion internal combustion vehicles, or as coal in power stations, or in other industry uses, or farmers burning stubble, or loggers burning forests, and when wildfires add to all these products of combustion, we are polluting the air and robbing it of oxygen. But heat will kill us long before oxygen runs out. To repeat, as a result of **what we burn** our species and millions of other species may go extinct.

We not only have to URGENTLY restore the stabilizing functions of the biosphere, but (I regret to say) we will have to seriously consider how to *consciously* geoengineer our way out of all the damage we've done – and which we are STILL making worse – so that we can hopefully restore the benign liveability of Spaceship Earth for our children and for all our hoped-for descendants. However, if we *do* try to slow global heating by some technical intervention, then it cannot be what anti-extinction activist, Ben See, correctly characterizes as 'buying time for the Extinction Economy to keep destroying'. We cannot simply prolong our current industrial, Nature-destruction economy; we MUST make our livelihood *within* the ecological constraints, *aka* the carrying capacity, or biocapacity, of Spaceship Earth.

The term **Spaceship Earth** indicates a world-view encouraging everyone to act as a member of a harmonious spaceship crew working toward the greater good. The term's earliest use was in a sentence in Henry George's 1879 book *Progress and Poverty*. It was also inferred in a 1965 speech by US politician Adlai Stevenson. It was coined by British-American economist Kenneth Boulding (1910–1993), a peacenik and one of many founders of ecological economics, who used the phrase in the title of his 1966 essay, "The Economics of the Coming Spaceship Earth" in which he wrote of the need for our economic systems to fit with the global ecological system. The phrase was again used by Buckminster Fuller (1895–1983) in his 1968 book *Operating Manual for Spaceship Earth*. This is a quote where Fuller cautions against the sudden over-use of Earth's vast-time geological energy savings in the form of fossil fuels:

> *We can make all of humanity successful through science's world-engulfing industrial evolution provided that we are not so foolish as to continue to exhaust in a split second of astronomical history*

the orderly energy savings of billions of years' energy conservation aboard our Spaceship Earth.

Forward thinking people like Schumacher, Boulding and Fuller could see that we were about to burn all that stored energy as quickly as possible, but that little good might come of it in the longer term.

Despite the fantasies of billionaires like Musk (SpaceX), Bezos (Blue Origin), and Branson (Virgin Galactic), who might have been inspired by the 1976 book *The High Frontier: Human Colonies in Space* by Gerard K. O'Neill, we cannot thrive in outer space. We evolved in Earth's biosphere and apart from our inborn need to remain at one with it, there is the fact that the atmosphere shields us from deadly cosmic radiation, keeps us at liveable temperatures, and gives us oxygen to breathe. Space colonists would need pressurized, humidified and heated lead boxes to travel and to live in. Not to mention all the food and water that Earth provides. Cocoa trees, for chocolate, don't grow on Mars.

Instead of dreams of a cosmos-sized colonial project, the term 'Spaceship Earth' gives us the sense of Earth's biosphere as the living quarters of our one-and-only spaceship, for which we are responsible. This, I believe, is actually the single best thing to come out of all our space exploration – a genuine planetary consciousness. The sooner we decide to accept our terrestrial limitations, the sooner we will put all our efforts into caring for it. For certain we cannot thrive anywhere else. We cannot thrive on the moon or Mars. Venus is what happens when there's runaway global heating. The limits of space travel for the human body have probably already been reached. The best and biggest dividend of all our space programs could be in acquiring **spaceship thinking** where we fully understand that we are aboard a finite, closed-loop, self-sustaining, space-traveller that we call Earth. Then we can become rational inner-space travelers and learn to live on, take care of, and love Spaceship Earth in peace and friendly co-operation. There is no Planet B.

However, the surface of Earth is heating itself and the heating is accelerating (via Albedo loss, released carbon-dioxide, methane, etc). We must now try to restore the heat balance so the heat gain slows and eventually stops. But more than that, we must encourage it to slowly lose heat for a while because all the heat it has gained, and will yet unavoidably gain, especially in the oceans, is not compatible with the healthy living conditions that all the species of the biosphere require. Without our concerted and clever action now, this sixth mass extinction will be a lot worse than any of the five before it.

All this means we must take RADICAL climate action – like stopping all emissions and actively helping Nature to restore herself. She can no longer do it by herself, even if all we humans die out, and go extinct this century. Of course the many countless deaths from global heating and wars have well and truly started, ***but we're not dead yet!*** There are many things we CAN do to slow global heating. Denial and inaction CANNOT be permitted options because both are anti-survival; they may be the ultimate maladaptive behaviours.

To begin with, we need 'degrowth' or fair economic contraction; i.e. economics for need, not greed. And even though our whole economy runs on fossil fuels, we must stop mining and burning them. That will mean urgent electrification and fuel rationing as we drop emissions as fast as possible and try to draw down CO_2, CH_4 and other greenhouse gases from the atmosphere. De-globalisation, localism, anti-consumerism, and product-austerity will be needed (we rich folks have to stop buying stuff we don't need). We must have laws against Ecocide in every country. And we need an international environment treaty whereby all nations commit to restoring Nature. All this must lead to world peace so we can stop all our polluting, wasteful, suicidal militarism and war-making. We can also strictly minimise flying and go vegetarian as much as possible. These things we can do as local, national, and global communities. We must stop all logging and deforestation NOW and plant trillions of fast-growing trees (perhaps not flammable eucalypts, as much as I love gum trees).

We must ban all plastics and substitute every plastic use with a biodegradable or reusable alternative. Food, water and shelter security must be everyone's top priorities. We can stop all our pollution before it reaches the ocean, filtering every outfall, and require all the chemical companies to stop adding toxins to their products. Another thing we must do is restore the Albedo effect by making every available surface (i.e. everything that's not a growing plant) reflective/white. The polar ice sheets are so depleted and diminishing that they are making the heating of the globe even more rapid than climate scientists expected. We must have MERA – Make Everything Reflective Again. This kind of passive **geo-engineering** will be cost-effective and cause minimal harm in the long run. Of course we will be forced to convert all military personnel to emergency workers and shut down all military outfits because, whether we take survival action or not, the biggest struggle globally will be in reacting to climate catastrophes, and for that we need human resources too.

In the words of UN Secretary General, António Guterres: *Every country must be part of the solution. Demanding others move first only ensures humanity comes last.* Guterres added that the IPCC calls for a number of other actions including: no new coal, oil or gas; the phasing out of coal by 2030 in OECD countries and as soon as possible in all other countries; ending all public subsidies and private funding of coal, oil, and gas; ensuring net zero electricity generation by 2035 for all developed countries, and as soon as possible for the rest of the world; ceasing all licensing, approvals or funding of new coal, oil and gas; stopping any expansion of existing fossil fuel reserves; shifting all subsidies from fossil fuels to a just energy transition; and establishing a global phase down of existing fossil fuel production compatible with the 2050 global net zero emissions target. Can we cool the planet? Maybe, IF we act now. Here's an American documentary that discusses some of this.

>https://www.youtube.com/watch?v=PeYJTluQ5tM

NUCLEAR? YEAH NAH!

There's an L/NP push to delay or stop our transition to renewable energy. This attack on our well-being is despite the fact that renewable energy is by far the cheapest and most environmentally friendly of all sources of electricity. The 2024 Liberal leader, Peter Dutton, plus most News Corp 'hosts' and others, have been claiming that nuclear power is the cheapest source of electricity. It is simply not plausible that Mr Dutton could be that ignorant and actually believes that Nukes are cheaper – not even Mr Dutton could be that ignorant of the facts, so he must be lying. How are he, the L/NP and News Corp gaining from such lies? They must be calculating that a lie repeated often enough will convince some people that it's true. That's the tactic Joseph Goebbels used in WWII and which Trump, Netanyahu and News Corp keep using – lie, and lie, and lie again. That's the tactic that worked for Dutton and the 'No' campaign during the Voice referendum, so no doubt the L/NP and News Corp expect it to work in the next federal election. See here for the Big lie:

>https://en.wikipedia.org/wiki/Big_lie
>https://www.bing.com/search?q=goebbels+quote+if+you+tell+a+lie+big+enough&FORM=QSRE1

Lying about how good nuclear energy is only serves the liar's purpose, not ours. We need honesty, truth and fact-checking at every turn if we are going to survive. So yes, renewable energy harvesting *does* have detrimental effects on Nature, but those are nothing compared to the thousands of years of contamination by radio-nuclides that were never found in Nature. And renewables arguably have the smallest environmental effect among all our energy collecting systems and are much superior for powering our technological civilization. Wind and solar schemes can be integrated with agricultural land use and even assist by providing shade for livestock and power for moving water to where it can aid plant growth. Tidal and wave will soon add to the mix. Plus, those who support the complicated and expensive technology of fission-based nuclear energy from our limited and hard-to-mine supply of heavy metals (uranium *et al*) are ignoring the fact that solar energy is virtually unlimited fusion-based nuclear energy that is cheap to harvest and available to all. Maybe that's the problem that the 'conservatives' have with renewable energy, it's available to everyone who has a means to collect it, and therefore it can cancel all corporate capitalist profiteering in the delivery of energy. In truth, the sun, wind and tides are just too damn egalitarian-democratic, small-folk friendly, and liberation-socialist in character for the pirate-profiteers!

Dutton says his centralised, government-funded nuclear power stations won't need new transmission lines, like some big renewable schemes might do, because he can plug into the existing (market-oriented) electricity grid. Even if that's true, the huge costs and risks of nuclear plants are still far greater than the cost of new (underground) transmission lines. But, when every home and business has its own solar system and batteries there will be much less need for transmission lines. Decentralized, independent, and domesticated electricity supplies are more democratic, more resistant to climate disasters, and they liberate us from dependence on the profiteering business model of the energy marketeers we have now.

A quick word about the Small Modular (Nuclear) Reactors (SMRs) that the L/NP sometimes talks of: it's not only that they're unproven and uneconomical, but the telling point is that these SMRs are intended to be more flexible by heating molten salt in order to store energy and to release it when needed (unlike the inflexible big nukes that have to drive steam turbines day and night), yet Solar Thermal Energy with towers and mirror-fields can do the same job with simpler, cheaper, and less-polluting technology:

https://en.wikipedia.org/wiki/Solar_thermal_energy

While maliciously organizing anti-renewable rallies, the L/NP also plan to put huge amounts of public money into nuclear power instead of investing in our switch to the cheapest and cleanest electricity production option, and the most efficient consumption option, namely, full electrification. This complete absurdity must have an ulterior motive. The most obvious sneaky-reason is that nuclear-fission reactors for generating electricity would give Australia a nuclear industry that would also produce nuclear-weapons-grade products (and trained technicians) in support of American's Nuclear War Triad that the AUKUS submarines, B-52s and long-range missiles are planned to be part of.

Nuclear power plants are too slow to build and too expensive. CSIRO said so – for the technically-minded, the 2023 GenCost report:

GenCost: cost of building Australia's future electricity needs

The nuclear fission required to make heat for the steam turbines leaves radioactive products that have long, but various half-lives. Some decay quickly, but some must be managed for up to 100,000 years, which is humanly impossible. The result is that any further nuclear proliferation will only add to the toxic legacy of global radioactive pollution, which, added to all our plastic, the PFAS chemicals (per and poly-fluoroalkyl substances), and other bio-toxic pollutants, is as much committing genocide on our own children as is the accelerating global heating that we are doing so little about. Why do Right-wing people *hate their own children* so much as to want *more* crumbling nuclear facilities and radioactive waste for all our children to deal with, and adding this to a world that's heating too fast for life to be sustained?

But they may yet leave this lethal legacy. The young are being gulled into the false notion that nukes are benign, and being given a false sense of security about the resilience of Earth's biosphere. Everyone who is younger than 40 years of age can only remember the Fukushima disaster of 2011. Young people won't remember the **terror** of the Cold War when the danger of Nuclear Armageddon was nearing its worst. And they won't remember all the atmospheric testing of nuclear weapons that contaminated the whole planet and marked the geological start of the **Anthropocene** in 1950. And young people won't understand that the danger of nuclear war will never go away until there are no more nukes in the world. The danger is still very much with us, with its flawed MAD deterrence doctrine, and the mad power-lust that keeps the nuclear weapons states clinging to their weapons of mass murder. It's this vicious spiral of insanity that the pro-nuclear advocates want to drag us into by nuclearising Australia. As of January 2024 there were about 12,100 nuclear warheads in the world. Over 3,000 are deployed at high operational alert, mostly by the US and Russia. Those two countries still hold most of the world's nuclear weapons at over 5,000 each while China has only four to five hundred non-deployed warheads. Israel has over ninety nuclear weapons. The number has at least been reduced from its 1985 peak of about 63,600 warheads. The United Nations treaties aimed at preventing nuclear war include the Non-Proliferation of Nuclear Weapons Treaty (NPT), the Comprehensive Nuclear Test Ban Treaty (CTBT), and the Treaty on the Prohibition of Nuclear Weapons (TPNW). For the TPNW we can thank the International Campaign to Abolish Nuclear weapons (ICAN) which was founded in Melbourne and won the 2017 Nobel Peace Prize.

Our young people won't remember, or understand, the great nuclear disasters like Three Mile Island, Chernobyl or even Fukushima. They will even be too young to remember the Montreal Protocol which sort-of saved us from terminal Ozone loss in 1987. In one of her many books, *Nuclear Power Is Not The Answer to Global Warming or Anything Else* (2006) Dr Helen Caldicott (1938–present) lays out the case against nuclear power. Dr Caldicott also worries that memories of nuclear disasters are fading. The International Nuclear and Radiological Events Scale (INES), rates nuclear accidents on a logarithmic scale of 1 to 7. At level 5 and above, the consequences are impossible to remove from the biosphere. Here is a list of seven such accidents:

12th December 1952	Ontario, Canada, INES Level 5
29th September 1957	Mayak, Kyshtym, Russia, INES Level 6
10th October 1957	Sellafield (*aka* Windscale), Cumberland, UK, INES Level 5
21st January 1969	Lucens, Vaud, Switzerland, INES Level 5
28th March 1979	Three Mile Island, Pennsylvania, USA, INES Level 5
26th April 1986	Chernobyl, Ukraine, INES Level 7
11th March 2011	Fukushima, Japan, INES Level 7

There have been many other accidents with less global effect (most are military accidents that have been kept largely secret), but, sadly, those major nuclear disasters won't be the last before we eventually rid ourselves of the whole poisonous nuclear industry.

Nuclear power causes a lot of CO_2 emissions in mining, transport and refining of the uranium ore. Nuclear power needs expensive, high-tech facilities that really only heat water to drive steam turbines to turn electricity generators. So it has many safety concerns. It needs huge government (public money) support. A nuclear industry is essential for making nuclear weapons, and the nuclear cycle produces radioactive chemicals that can escape into our food chain and into the air we breathe. These chemicals cause DNA damage, cancers and other life-shortening illnesses. Radioactive waste needs long-term storage so it won't poison people. So far, the politicians, nuclear scientists and technologists don't know what to do with this waste. It is *worse* than unfair and immoral to leave our descendants with the responsibility for our radioactive pollution – it is downright criminal.

In July 2024, Gina Rinehart held back-to-back fundraisers for L/NP leader Peter Dutton (the man whom Malcolm Turnbull dubbed 'a thug'). This shows that Dutton's nuclear push isn't about energy – it's partly about helping billionaires like Gina Rinehart (whose father stole most of the iron in the Kimberley) and partly about keeping coal and gas burning for decades to come. Dutton has tried to tie his nuclear push to the rising cost of living, but he admits that public money would have to bear the full cost and risk of any nuclear reactors because there is no business case for them and no private investors will touch them. Plus, as renewables are cheaper than fossil fuels, the miners and energy companies can see their fossil fuels becoming stranded assets. Soon both uranium and fossil fuels won't be worth digging up – which will be great for the environment – but that's why the fossil-fuel/uranium-mining cabal is doing all it can to expand now while there's still some profiteering to be had. It is said that in 2023, seven percent of global GDP went to fossil fuel subsidies. If we simply stopped this enormous amount of public money going toward worsening atmospheric pollution, then we would have a much better chance of slowing climate change.

CLIMATE CHANGE AGAIN

Few people would deny a finding by the whole field of medical science that they're on course to certain death from cancer and that business-as-usual is simply not an option if they are to have the slimmest chance of postponing their death. But, when the whole field of Earth sciences (and the UN) tells them the grimmest truth regarding the inevitable and imminent extinction of humans, then there are plenty of politicians, media identities, and fossil-fuel shills insisting the scientists are all liars and that business-as-usual must never be slowed at any cost. Few stop to think that 50 kilometres above our heads the temperature is nearly *minus* 273° C, yet the wonderful protective blanket that we all breathe has kept Earth's average temperatures benign enough for long enough for ourselves and millions of other species to evolve. Climate science deniers aggressively deny the terminal prognosis for humans from heat driven climate disasters, but they can't make it untrue.

As stated at the beginning, it's grievous that our education system virtually ignored the threat of global warming even though the physics was known since 1856. Scientists in the oil companies knew the problem in 1967. ExxonMobil denied it after 1977. Here's Carl Sagan explaining the Greenhouse Effect and Climate Change very carefully in 1985:

> https://www.youtube.com/watch?v=Wp-WiNXH6hI

That so many people, over so many decades, have not been taught the physics of global heating, and that consequently the climate-deniers did, and still can, get away with sowing doubt, is horrendous. Honestly, the ecological collapse we've set in motion is frightening. Most of us don't want to live with that fear, so we usually block out the truth. To put it another way, the science-denying, fear-mongering Murdoch media (or as propagandist Edward Bernays put it, our 'invisible government') missed a top chance to provoke fear by *not* telling the truth about global heating. The time when it's really important to recall the truth is when we go to vote. Our best hope is in electing politicians who are not afraid of News Corp and not in the pay of the fossil fuel corporations.

GLOBAL HEATING SOLUTIONS?

Denial is no use to anyone. We MUST acknowledge that ecosystems are collapsing and that it's our economy that is the primary cause. There are many things we *can* do to slow the heating. We need a science-based, well-publicized plan coming from communities *and* governments. A global climate treaty is a top priority. Initially, we can start by applying passive tactics that fall short of active geo-engineering – which is rapidly becoming more necessary. As outlined, these actions include deliberate and shared slowing of everything so there's benign contraction or 'degrowth'; making our economic system fair and for need, not greed; phasing out the burning of fossil fuels and going fully electric as fast as possible; restoring the Albedo effect by making everything that isn't green and growing turn white/reflective; establishing an international environment treaty which includes plastics and all toxic chemicals; developing laws against ecocide to protect and restore Nature; stopping all militarism and wars and making World Peace; minimising flying to essentials only (much less tourism); stopping all deforestation; reducing our population benignly with family planning and voluntary contraception (two child limit per fertile woman); using many fewer cars (ICE or EV); improving public transport; making much more soil; reducing food waste; growing our own food; applying regenerative agricultural techniques; being mostly vegetarian; rewilding land where appropriate; protecting ocean plankton, krill, all biota, and growing trillions of trees!

A silver-lining thought is that as the CC damage increases it may soon spur enough motivation for the majority of people to get behind these vitally necessary changes.

REGARDING THAT CULTURAL MOTIVATION

Genesis, the first book of The Bible, tells humans to subdue the Earth and go forth and multiply. Global heating gives us no choice but to stop wrecking the Earth and stop multiplying without limit. We must repudiate Genesis 1:28 with all our hearts and actions. We must also repudiate the actions of all those who wish to continue the suicidal madness of growth-without-end capitalism. None of our imagined gods are going to save us, so we must also insist on rationality over 'religious' lies and delusion. This demands a huge cultural reversal. With apologies, here's a shortened quote from an author whom I was unable to identify:

> *To be useful, economics must focus **not** on extracting maximum profit from minimum expenditure, but on providing services for all according to their need. We need to harness new technologies, but only with the aim of sustainable survival, not for the profits of the few. We need to support science. We need to commit to the local, national, and global mission of sustainable living, while also fostering a meaningful cultural environment. The neoliberal era, which has squeezed the last ounces of billionaire profit from the dying system, is now over.*

The only remaining question is whether we let civilization collapse by refusing to overhaul our economic framework, or undertake a complete and radical socio-cultural-economic reformation.

While I'm not trying to spruik for my unpublished book, I try to address this socio-cultural-economic 'reformation' in *Liberation Economics* where there is more room for long discussion. I confess, this booklet has a sour, trenchant tone, but in the larger book, I try to show how this reformation must be loving, kind and peaceful in character. This is because we are unlikely to survive if we don't learn to love one another, to make peace with all our so-called enemies, and above all to love Nature, the living biosphere of Spaceship Earth on which all our lives depend. To create this reformation for our survival, we need to engage both our minds and hearts, which is why I propose a philosophy of panphilism – a love of all living things. Only with applied love, or at least care, will we get our attitudes straight. And we need truth, rationalism, and science, but we also need heart-felt care, kindness, understanding, empathy and co-operation. Care is love in action. So in order to save Nature and ourselves we need the utmost *care* – for the world and for one another.

Very briefly, regarding care, and in searching for a better narrative, I've arrived at an idea I call **Panphilism** – love of everything, loving one another, and loving life. To clarify a little, Panphilism is where rational Humanist-altruism meets the emotional element of Deep Ecology. It's a science-respecting 'religio' (right living) with a biophilia sentiment. It's not a practice or a dogma, and there's nothing to worship. (What sort of god is it that needs worshiping?) Like Deep Ecology, it is a way of relating to all species and Nature with heart-felt sensitivity. There's an indispensible concept that is held as a virtue in Jainism, Buddhism, Hinduism and Sikhism, and that's the practice of non-violence or *ahimsa* written अहिंसा in Sanskrit. I believe that is what Jesus was trying to teach, 500 years after Buddhism was founded. For example, 'turn the other cheek' Matthew 5:39 and 'love your enemies' Matthew 5:44. Panphilism fits with Atheist Quakerism and a suite of the atheist religions including Taoism, Shinto, Jainism, Buddhism, and Confucianism.

Here I can mention that the *Liberation* part of my larger book has the dual sense of emancipation from poverty and inequality, but is also focused on a liberating cultural reformation. One quote that is attributed to Greta Thunberg says this:

> ... the climate crisis is not just about the environment. It is a crisis of human rights, of justice, and of political will. Colonial, racist, and patriarchal systems of oppression have created and fueled it. We need to dismantle them all.

I believe that a cultural reformation can change all our systems for the better. And such a cultural reformation is key to our transition/liberation out of the ways we have been living and towards the ways in which Nature and science are telling us we must live, if we are to survive. Living as if we care for the world and one another requires a new Enlightenment – in the realms of both knowledge and emotion. We need the full engagement of both hearts and minds if we are going to achieve that permanent greenpeace.

The religious or right-living 'enlightenment' was best described by philosophies that arose in India and grew in China and wider Asia. (Imperialist Europe and Russia have been too belligerent for it until now.) A Sanskrit word for it is *moksha* (मोक्ष), which is a term in Hinduism, Jainism, Buddhism, and Sikhism for various experiences of liberation, or nirvana (or perhaps as Jesus taught regarding 'the kingdom of heaven'). Moksha is freedom from ignorance. It is also self-knowledge and self-actualization. We need liberation from our old ways in order to become enlightened crew members of Spaceship Earth. And we cannot make the world our good place (eutopia) unless we change a lot of things. This is *not* suggesting a new monism, just a very necessary and broad cultural evolution.

It must be said that having only one world religion, like having only one political or economic dogma (e.g. neoliberal capitalism), would be both boring and very prone to error. Rather, it's better to have as many paths to spiritual solace as there are people. Just as everyone has a unique fingerprint, so too could each have a unique religious or world view, or else no view. Not just kindly accepting differences but positively embracing pluralism is much more likely to maximize social harmony and everyone's happiness.

However I've identified a fifth existential threat that is a very old culturally acquired maladaptive behaviour, and which oddly magnifies the combining threats of global heating, economic growth, militarism, and nuclear weapons – it is deity belief.

Now, I must emphatically assert that everyone is free to believe whatever they want to in their own home – no question – but I'm sorry to have to tell you, **there is no god**. There is no deity that will help any of us; there is only love. That's to say, love between sentient beings.

There probably should be a word for the search for a deity which is neither mysticism (the endeavour to be at one with the ultimate cause of existence) nor theology which is more about comparative pantheons. That search, whatever it might be called, led me to atheist altruism – a sort of universal love, a love of life and of the connectedness between all species on this magical orb that we call our home. Of course we cannot love war and murdering, toxic chemicals and pollution, and many other human activities, but we can care about the people who commit such wrongs and we can care about all the people and other species who suffer from these wrongs. Someone said, 'Oh, you mean god is love.' Well no, because if we are talking about love then why try to call it something else, or give it one of the names of your thousands of imagined deities. No, love is love. And I think it's up to each of us to seek out how it operates in our lives and in the much wider biosphere of life.

As an aside, the ancient Greeks had a number of words for love: *Agápe* meaning to want the best for one another. *Philia* which may mean egalitarian respect – perhaps it's recalling the French Revolution cry, "liberté, égalité, fraternité" where fraternité means brotherly love; then there's *Éros*, meaning sexual passion. And there's *Philautia* meaning self-love such as what Trump, Tate, and similar onanists and narcissists are addicted to. Of course this is not a complete list, but it suffices to say there are many terms for love. Maybe the one that resonates best with panphilism is *Agápe* in the sense of a continuously reciprocal and respectful altruism, or as someone put it long ago, 'Love one another' (John 13:34).

As said above, care is love in action. Loving or caring for one another, and trying to love our so-called enemies, may seem to be beyond many of us as we watch the callous, cynical and hate-filled wars that are going on now, but I sincerely believe that only loving-care, *aka* loving kindness, will help us work our way out of our difficulties – if we apply it.

Speaking of the vital need for care and kindness, there is no escaping the fact that if we want a functioning civilization, then public servants, politicians, and policy-makers have a clear duty to adhere to the most truthful knowledge available to us, which means our science.

Our leaders must be secular rationalists, and we need enough rational secular voters to vote in such leaders. Although this may surprise some people, it is belief in a deity that is the other major threat to human survival. There are some major reasons for this: firstly, if people actually believe their deity is the only true god, then this gives them delusions of exceptionalism. That's the notion that one's doctrine/culture/belief-system is exceptional and superior to all others. This sets up the likelihood of conflict against anyone who imagines an alternative deity. The delusion of superiority leads people to dehumanise others and not see them as equally human. It's another expression of the toxic tribalism that our species indulges in. I give you just four examples of this murderous, faith-based, tribal and racist intolerance: first, the 200 years of Christian Crusades; next, how Zionists have treated Palestinians since 1948; also the violence of Salafi jihadism; and, of course, the Nazi Holocaust/Shoah. What these violent episodes have in common is that religionist beliefs of cultural/racial superiority and exceptionalism were used to fuel and excuse the violence by the self-righteous group against the oppressed people who were considered inferior by that oppressor. SO many horrors have been committed over whose the superior culture is, and who has the most real sky-ghost. But there is no god, and we must stop pretending there is. Religion-based exceptionalism has driven countless pointless murders and immeasurable needless suffering. It doesn't have to be that way.

Next, and maybe worst of all is if people actually believe there is a deity and/or another world beyond this-here-now, then they are not going to accept climate science. If deity-believers doubt or deny the science, then they won't help us adapt to or fight the heating, and they may actively oppose the urgent transition we must make.

Another important reason why our leaders must be non-theists is because 'believers' are prone to fatalism; they're likely to say 'god willing' and then do nothing, expecting that whatever happens was somehow meant to be. It's a very seductive way of thinking, but it's a direct path to disaster. If we throw up our hands and do nothing about global heating, then we are certainly doomed. We can't let fatalism give us, or anyone else, an excuse for inaction. So, once again I'm sorry, but we'll all have to leave our deity delusions at home for the duration of the global heating disaster – and that's likely to be thousands of years yet.

It's not a sign of a weak mind to believe in a deity. Even very intelligent people can compartmentalise the subjects they think about and may be very clever in one area while leaving other subjects 'on the shelf' of previous teaching or unexamined assumptions. We often work in metaphorical silos, and most of us store our knowledge in separate mental compartments, smart about some issues but dodging around or ignorant of others. But those unexamined assumptions leave us gullible and prey to the mendacious. In my opinion, many pastors and clerics are mendacious, telling lies to deceive vulnerable or gullible minds though some may believe what they preach. Children are easy prey, but older people can be sucked in too if they allow themselves to be. Among the worst are the Jimmy Swaggart types and similar 'televangelists' who tell lies and put on a performance of piety only to rake in money. As happened to Frank Houston, their corruption and hypocrisy is usually revealed sooner or later (Matthew 7:15). At the extreme end of gullibility, we see people so welded to the delusion that theirs is the one true deity that they will murder others on behalf of their own deity belief. Killing to prop up your god delusion is a whole other pathology.

Admittedly, many people find it comforting to mentally have a 'pocket deity' such as Jesus or Muhammad – a bit like a glorified St Christopher medallion, the ones that were popular to supposedly keep travellers from harm. There are plenty of minor deities, some of which were historical people and many others that are imaginary. What they all have in common is that they are tiny and very human compared with the scale of the real Universe. And any so-called heaven or hell only exists right here now. Our only heavenly haven-home is right before our eyes in the beauty and generosity of Nature, yet not enough people see this. And of course hell is the wars we inflict upon one another.

It seems to me that people who believe in any of the 'supreme deities' simply haven't thought about it clearly enough and/or for long enough. What I mean by 'thinking clearly' (about any of the deity theories) is not just being rational and logical but also meditating on the non-rational. There is far more to life and death than we yet realise. There is a spiritual and mystical side to this heavenly world, which we ignore at our loss, but ultimately there is no deity to save us from ourselves. What the deist religions imagine does not exist. Any such icon is only an ancient yet tenacious day-dream. It's curious how so many people talk as if there is a god but behave as if there isn't. Yes, people do telepathically experience a 'superconsciousness', but that is our collective subconsciousness, the human 'hive-mind', and we often mistake it for something else. Mental telepathy is real and functioning, but many of us have shut it off by adulthood, just as we have shut off empathy and loving-kindness (as his holiness Tenzin Gyatso, the 14th Dalai Lama calls it) because our objectivist-capitalist culture denies these things. But it's very important to be aware of our hive-mind and of our deeper, more subtle consciousness, because it is through those that media propagandists, demagogues, and political and religious leaders can manipulate us.

(Telepathy is poorly researched, and so is intuition – knowing things at a distance in time and space. One thing I learnt as a nurse is that we ignore our intuition at our peril.)

Self-evidently, we must have rational secularists as our leaders and policy-makers so they will make decisions based on scientific reality, not on any deity myth. And, as I said, we need enough educated voters to vote in science-literate leaders. There are up to twenty reasons why we must drop our gods (which I detail in my larger book). One that relates to economics is the ridiculous 'Prosperity Gospel' theory that if you're rich or poor it's because an imaginary god made you that way – which gives the believer a perfect excuse to chase money, lionise the rich, excuse inequality, ignore poverty, and punch down on the poor. Such 'Christians' could not have read, *It is easier for a camel to go through the eye of a needle than for a rich man to see heaven.* (Matthew 10:25, & 19:24, plus Luke 18:25.)

And here's another way in which 'believing' is a danger: if a leader convinces themselves they are being guided by whatever deity they imagine, and if they believe their sky-ghost is omnipotent and omniscient, then they are likely to make any sort of crazy decision and to believe they and their decisions to be always right and blessed – regardless of anything. Australia saw all this play out in the behaviours of the misogynist and classist PM Morrison whose Pentecostal millennialism allowed him to deny climate science and to smirkingly facilitate the very same fossil fuel industry that's driving us to the end of our world.

This theory of a god-ordained leader was based on the (conservative) St Paul's assertion in Romans 13:1–2 that we have to obey 'the powers that be'. Consequently, we get conceited and self-righteous leaders who can convince many people that they're always right. When a leader supposedly has god-given power, the power of the state is seen as continuous with that of the dictator and the deity, and all three are unquestionable. Hence we have 'the divine right of kings'; so Hitler was seen as the rightful Führer of the Motherland; Putin's death squads and war crimes are blessed by the Patriarchs of the Russian Christian church; or the Christian-exceptionalist (IN GOD WE TRUST) American military/espionage complex believes its meddling in hundreds of other countries is its manifest destiny, and Israelis believe Netanyahu's murderous IDF is fulfilling the god-given destiny of the Zionist State.

This side of the deity delusion takes us to where people believe bizarre nonsense such as that thousands of years ago their 'deity' gave them a certain patch of 'holy' land to live on exclusively. Or equally delusional, that this deity lived as a singular anti-establishment male/preacher 2,000 years ago, got executed by the authorities, but is still alive today and making his followers immortal. Or that 1,400 years ago the same deity (by a different name) wanted his followers to kill people who didn't believe in the fairy story of his existence.

St. Paul's authority-directive (Romans 13:1–2) was made by a conservative (Paul), and it suits the conservative mind to obey the powers that be. Maybe that's why conservatives don't want Australia to be a democratic republic but prefer to retain the hierarchical authority structure of England's hereditary monarchy. Cromwell refuted that in 1649.

None of this is radically anti-religion. For example, despite the fact that *in my opinion* Saul of Tarsus misrepresented the Buddhist teachings of Yeshua bar Yosef and invented a false, super-scapegoat narrative that persists to this day in the various Christian sects, I have much respect for Jorge Mario Bergoglio (now known as Pope Francis). I think Francis sets an example of trying, in a heart-felt way, to express himself as the best person he can be. And although I'd disagree with his theology (after all, it's well proven that life on Earth evolved itself, so there's no such thing as creation or a creator-god), Pope Francis is totally right in what he says in his environmentalist encyclicals, *Laudato si'* (2015) and *Laudate Deum* (2023). I disagree with the pontiff that it's a deity that we've turned away from – I'd say it's loving-kindness, compassion and empathy that we are lacking. But I certainly agree that many of our problems are based in our tendency to objectify everything, which causes us not to **care** enough and to trash Nature, one another, and other living beings, as if nothing matters. We have a cancer in our civilization called *capitalist nihilism*. Our whole consumer society and linear economy is based on taking from Nature, making stuff and then wasting it. It would be great if a lot more of the faithful would read these works and absorb the urgent message that Francis has been trying to convey about global heating, its causes and our much-needed responses.

We can and should be respectful of one another's sincerely held beliefs, but we can agree to disagree. Cultural diversity is a great strength to a population. Monocultures tend to be inflexible, more closed, and ill-equipped to change and adapt. The large monotheisms such as Judaism, Christianity, and Islam each have millions of sincere followers who are harmless while ever they don't try to impose their beliefs on others. Along with all other religions, they have followers who are kind, caring, and who love to do good work. Unfortunately, there are also a few militant and aggressive elements in all the big monotheisms. Any society is well served by diversity, but we must keep religion out of politics. Deity-believers are welcome to debate me on the need for rational secularism in politics.

Religions and philosophies are responses to the need for awe, understanding, and heart-felt connection that seems to exist in all sentient animals. It's easily enough perceived in elephants, cetaceans, and we larger primates. We see this need in our pets, dogs, horses and others who all need the love and connectedness we exchange with them. The etymology of 'religion' is from old Latin *religare*, to bind. It seems intuitively obvious that we need to revitalise our connections to Nature, and to one another, if we are going to take the next step in civilising ourselves – i.e. making world peace and rescuing Earth's life-support systems. Philosophies and religions can help us deal with grief, loss, joy, love, expressing compassion and conceiving meaning in our lives. They help us to work out how to live good lives, cultivate ourselves and make ourselves kinder.

Where the dangers come from in many religions is in those delusions of superiority, exceptionalism, and infallibility. That's why it's vital to keep the belligerent, authoritarian, and proselytising sort of religion *way* out of politics. As I explain in my book, freedom *from* religion should be enshrined in Article 18 of the Universal Declaration of Human Rights along with freedom *of* religion. The separation of church and state, and radically secular government, are indispensable principles born out of bitter experience. Yet we still see so-called theocracies where the clerics act like a military junta. Plus we get chauvinist-nationalist movements such as Israeli Zionism, jihadist Salafism, the Hindu Rashtriya Swayamsevak Sangh, and American Christian Dominionism – all of which are inclined to supremacist delusions, dehumanizing out-groups, and often resort to violence.

More than just false notions of superiority, many deity believers have been wrongly taught, and believe, that this existence, this Earth, is a hell full of suffering and that there's a mythical paradise or heaven waiting for them when they die. That's nonsense, of course, but it has the effect of dragging many others into their cynical and maladaptive mindset. The real truth is that this planet is as near to being a heaven as we could even imagine. It is our only heavenly haven home and we do not have to live lives of suffering. Regrettably, we've polluted and abused the biosphere, and the war-makers make life hellish for everyone.

It's not religions per se that are maladaptive, but those that are deity-obsessed and aggressively intolerant. Religions and philosophies answer a need, so we need to respect sincere mental-emotional searching while not tolerating the intolerant, mind-controlling, cult-corporations – and having the wisdom to know the difference. Alarm bells should ring when a religion bans music or seeks to interfere in women's reproductive autonomy; if books are getting banned; if you hear nonsense terms like 'blasphemy' or 'apostasy'; or when a 'faith' becomes a cult, or another version of power-mad fascism. It's important to remember we are all in life's tragic-comedy together – we're all in the same boat – or on the same spaceship. There are many paths to the top of the mountain, and many spokes give strength to the wheel. We need to follow the more kind, peace loving, and Earth-friendly religions. These include the atheist religions and philosophies such as Jainism, Buddhism, Stoicism, Shinto, Taoism, Humanism, Deep Ecology – or invent your own.

You may ask why any of this matters. It matters because if we are going to save ourselves from global heating, then we have to minimize the theocratic denial of climate science and earth science – and we have to thoroughly repudiate Genesis 1:28. I'm fussing over this one archaic Biblical verse because it exemplifies the *attitude* that's foundational to exploitative, extractive capitalism. And if we are going to silence the arrogant, lying, vituperative attacks upon science by the extreme-Right (exemplified hideously by the deliberately-ignorant, cheerleader-shallow, performative-nastiness on Sky News in Australia), then we are going to have to defend rationality and truth at every turn.

Another issue is that if god is male, then male is god. So if we are going to get rid of the oppressive patriarchy, toxic masculinity, and male violence, then we also need to dethrone any notions of male supremacy, and that, in turn, means abolishing all the gods and particularly the male ones. There is no 'wise lord', no Ahura Mazda, no Zeus, Yahweh, Allah, God, or any other deity, and there never has been. (Of course there is not and never has been a Devil either!) I think Dante Alighieri expressed this well at the end of his 1321 poem, *Divine Comedy* (*Comedia*) – his ultimate revelation was of 'the Love which moves the sun and the other stars'. There is no deity, there is only love.

Percy Bysshe Shelley knew it too – see *Prometheus Unbound* where humanity (represented by Prometheus) finally stops feeding his emotional energy to the mythical deity, Jupiter (Zeus or any other deity name) then the deity, the imagined tyrant, loses its power and is extinguished in a flash of loving enlightenment and liberation. Shelley's thesis is that we can overthrow the tyrants, tyrannies, and maladaptive behaviours in our lives when we stop believing in them and thereby giving them our power. Whether it's a deity, a demigod, a demagogue, a monarch, a military junta, militarism itself, belligophilia, a corporation, a government, a tradition, or an ideology – they only have power because we, the people, give our power to them. None of the demagogues or tyrants have any power if they have no followers to enable them. The tendency toward a Nazi-style mindset is more prevalent in us than we care to admit, and many give way to it, but if we stop being enablers for unkind, lying, or corrupt people, war-makers, harmful traditions, erroneous economic systems, or any of our other stupidities, then they will each lose their power and vanish into history.

It's vital not to replace one tyranny with another. (For example when Lenin, contrary to Marxism, put the vanguard party and state-ownership at the centre of the omnipotent, omniscient state, he and Stalin started a line of tsar-like dictators that continues to this day.) A truly democratic society ensures that government and power are devolved and that needs are met where they are felt. Australia is suffering the tyranny of neoliberal meanness. With 3.3 million people living below the poverty line, it's obvious that our two-party duopoly is not a healthy democracy; it's not serving us well enough. The two-party system that's dominant in the Anglo-sphere has been trending toward a group-thinking, corporate-capitalist monopoly in every country where it's practised. China, as an effective one-party state, has out-performed the so-called democracies in almost every measure. (Sadly, their similar economic system has also created a lot of inequality in China.)

The actual existence of billionaires indicates a major flaw in our system. In recent years the world's tally of billionaires has been growing despicably, along with their obscene wealth. However, our democracies are being revived by a movement of innovators, diversity-embracing, heterodox thinkers, and independent politicians. Australians who have contributed to this disruption of the tyranny of the neoliberal political duopoly include people striving for integrity and truth such as Tony Windsor, Cathy McGowan, Andrew Wilkie, Barbara Pocock, the so-called Teal independents, David Pocock and many others. In the US, Bernie Sanders and Robert Reich stood out, and in the UK, Jeremy Corbyn tried to shift the dial. These are just a few of the many people who are resisting the tyranny of the dominant narrative of consumer capitalism. The point may be this: don't criticise another's tyranny or tyrants until you've examined and dethroned your own. (Matt 7:3–5, or Luke 6:41–42)

The rise of the Nazis in the Weimar Republic shows that, while a (small 'l') liberal democracy has to be tolerant (by definition), any society that hopes to survive cannot tolerate the intolerable. The Nazis spread hatred, vicious propaganda and lied shamelessly. They didn't care what was true as long as they contrived to get enough political power to crush the democracy. (Trumpism anyone?) The republic tolerated the hate and lies, so democracy was lost to the fanatical militarism and extreme racism of the Nazis. At present, Australia is tolerating main-stream lies and divisive propaganda coming from our commercial media. The lies polarise public opinion even further on social media. As I've said, the worst liars are the many News Corp outlets. Their lies are squarely aimed at sowing division, anger, and distrust – because these attract an audience for the advertising from which they get their profit. Their unjustified and persistent attacks on the ABC are one example. The fact that they keep denying climate science is another. They confected outrage when an experienced journalist mentioned the obvious fact of long-term racism in Australia. News Corp outlets have the hide to claim that Islamism is dividing Australia when it is actually their pro-American-militarist, Christian Dominionism that's really dividing us. The News Corp media are a threat to our democracy and to our social cohesion; Australia must not let the far-Right media do to us what they've done to the US or the UK, nor anything like what the Nazis did to Germany less than a hundred years ago.

The News Corp outlets have been shown to craft narratives, often quite untrue, just for the sake of keeping their audience and advertising profits. Ex-prime-ministers, Malcolm Turnbull and Kevin Rudd both regard the Murdoch's juggernaut as a threat to democracy in the US, UK, and Australia. Half a million Australians petitioned for a Royal Commission into the dominance of that (American) media magnate. All Murdoch outlets are a dual threat because they destabilise society and delay climate action. It's not just News Corp. All the commercial media are loose with the truth for reasons of profiteering, but News Corp has led the modern era in this blend of sensationalism, disinformation and political manipulation. It's likely that Rupert Murdoch studied the craft of 'tabloid' or 'yellow journalism' from William Randolph Hearst (See *Citizen Kane*, a 1941 film), but the Murdoch-owned Corporation has perfected the broadcast of anger, hate, and lies as a profitable art-form.

The L/NP-News Corp nexus maintains a stance that is strongly pro-American, pro-militarist, pro-Zionist and anti-China. Plus, mostly out of fear that News Corp will again demolish a Labor government, the ALP is not opposing that stance, even though the majority-world and the UN are recoiling in horror at the savagery of the what the Israeli-American military is doing in Gaza, Lebanon and most of Israel's neighbours. News Corp is causing Australia's Labor government to act against our best interests and to support the totally wrong side in global geo-politics. Israelis who once hunted Nazis after WWII have given way to an ultra-Zionist, murderous, war-loving, neo-Fascism that's starting WWIII, and it's NOT anti-Semitic to believe so. Australia is choosing war over of peace, profit over survival, death over life. News Corp is contriving to keep Australia in the far-right, capitalist orbit of the US-Israel-NATO hegemony.

The problem is that each of our large media corporations is effectively owned and controlled by one very rich individual. That person is able to set the political agenda for all the corporations' outlets and only those who conform to the boss's ideology are employed in those corporations. Thus the culture becomes entrenched and more extreme as time passes. Ultra-rich American men controlling our media include Murdoch, Musk, Bezos, Zuckerberg, and others. Governments become terrified of going against the ideology of the media bosses for fear of their company's persuasive power over large numbers of voters. This distorts and corrupts our democracy, but there is a way for it to be restored if a government has courage. Instead of supporting weapons industries the government could use its money and divestiture laws to break up monopolies (as meant for the Woolworths and Coles duopoly). The Murdoch machine can be compulsorily acquired (bought up), broken up, and all the media outlets given to the local ownership of community co-operatives. When each outlet is owned and operated by all the people of the community it serves, then there would be no incentive for them to publish misinformation or lies because their community would complain loudly if they did. The people will be able to speak for themselves.

Another facet of neo-fascism is that liberal-democratic Australia is presently tolerating intolerable things like shameless neo-Nazi white-supremacists, misogyny made popular, an epidemic of domestic violence and femicide, chronic poverty/inequality, an over-advertised rip-off gambling industry, and the continued parsimony of our corporate-captured, military-mad federal government. (Here's looking at you, Richard Marles.)

To elaborate: the zeitgeist of woman-hating, somewhat left-over from the L/NP era, has reached peak stupidity where boys abuse female teachers without any retributive consequences for those boys. They're aping the vile posturing of narcissistic, psychopathic animals such as Andrew Tate. There's little use in promoting positive, pro-equality male examples when some boys find Tate's violence more appealing. Young men get away with abusing women and easily avoid of any behaviour-rectifying painful retribution. I'm loath to talk like an aged, authoritarian-conservative, but boys who abuse female teachers need to suffer serious physical consequences so that their 'organism' learns such behaviours are totally forbidden. We cannot tolerate maladaptive behaviours such as racism, division, misogyny, femicide, and sexual or sectarian violence being normalised. Women are not objects for abuse and conquest. Males seeking dominance and 'victory' are just showing their weakness. Likewise we must reject macho militarism, the 'warrior' bullshit, and resist all rent-seeking war-profiteers, with every breath we take. The pathetic males of the so-called manosphere are simply putting their feelings of chronic inadequacy on show. Feelings of inadequacy are normal for male humans. Deal with it, mate! The sooks who whinge about women, and are afraid that women are rising up to having nearly equal rights, are just trying to drag women down again because they know they can't really compete. Well newsflash, you will never make yourself better by trying to diminish anyone else! From machismos who drive supersized trucks and muscle-headed Tate-types, to militarists who hide their fear inside a uniform, to femicidal men in Australia who are society's ultimate failures, and to the Taliban who are so very afraid of women that (since August 2024) they are demanding that no part of a woman be seen in public and even banning women's voices from being heard outside their prison/homes, the evidence is clear that these males (not 'men') are so stupidly and cravenly fearful of female power and women's competence that they actually belittle and imprison themselves. If you fellow males want to grow to be almost as good as most women, then you should take a long hard turn at doing 'women's work', and then you'll see what being a worthwhile human requires and you'll learn some proper respect!

And considering the step beyond disrespectful misogyny to Australia's epidemic of femicide, we need to re-educate males in order to prevent every sort of anti-female attitude. More urgently, we need many more safe shelters where women and children can escape from the evil, controlling males in their lives. This, too, is in the hands of our governments, who should be preparing each and every country for the really serious climate-induced problems to come. If we are going to cope with those, then gender-based disunity and men continuing to kill and abuse women is going to be extremely unhelpful.

Further to the above, we need to be working towards increasing **global unity** for the task of resisting global heating. Our best hope for this is the United Nations because it has some great philosophical foundations and is a well-established institution. Sadly, it has some flaws, most obvious of which is the veto powers of the five permanent members of the Security Council, the US, UK, Russia, France and China. This feature is a result of, and entrenches, the global power game as it stood at the end of WWII. From its first session in 1946, the superpower rivalries have continued to play out, and certainly France and Britain are only there as remnant colonial powers. The permanence and veto power of these nations needs to be abolished, but it's predictable that will be fiercely resisted. Also regrettably, a conglomeration of anti-UN conspiracy falsehoods has been spread by various paranoid people, notably the New World Order conspiracy theory which is afraid of a totalitarian world government. A moment's contemplation of the impossible logistics such a thing would require should dispel this lie. On the contrary, if we can merely increase international diplomacy and cooperation enough to achieve long overdue climate action, then that would be wonderful. At present UN Secretary-General António Guterres often sounds like a modern-day Cassandra, a voice of reason crying in the wilderness whose desperate calls for more climate action are being deliberately ignored. This is tragic because there are gigantic problems looming in coming decades as super-sized floods, fires, droughts, and storms disrupt our supplies of potable water and safe food.

WATER SECURITY

This is going to be increasingly important as we see not enough or too much water where we don't want either extreme. Obviously, keeping ourselves and our crops and homes away from flood damage is going to be vital. Equally, drought is a stealthy and merciless killer. At present there are more than 25 countries facing extreme water stress, and competition for fresh water leads to wars. But we live on a watery planet, so desalination and air-moisture harvesting are going to become huge new sectors as we fight to re-green deserts and barren lands. Fortunately, there are new technologies being developed. However, those original water cycle managers, the forests, need to be **urgently** restored and expanded.

FOOD SECURITY

We Australians are a bit spoiled. In our supermarkets we can get any kind of food, from any part of the globe, but if the fuels for farming and transport were stopped, most of us would go hungry. And if the ships stopped coming, we'd suddenly realise we have more people than we can provide good nutrition for. Sure, Australia is a net-exporter of food in the forms of wheat, beef, and other products of our American-style industrial agriculture, but so much of our varied diet is imported that we have effectively exceeded the carrying capacity of this land, and our economic system is largely to blame for that.

The way the relationship between city and country has evolved has meant that Nature's wealth is steadily being moved to the cities, and the power in fossil fuels accelerated that enormously since we left the horse and cart behind. A mainstay of that wealth-flow is that farmers are almost always price-takers, never price-setters. Buying on a seller's market and selling on a buyer's market creates a cost-price squeeze that makes farming a difficult job at the best of times. Weather events always made agriculture risky, but with global heating such events are becoming more extreme and more frequent. So, our biggest immediate threat is food insecurity. The first thing to do is have the proposed Australian Prices and Salaries Justification Authority (APASJA) ensure that farmers are getting a fair price for their produce and that consumers are not being ripped-off by the supermarket corporations. Professor Allan Fels, past ACCC chairman, has recommended new laws to give the commonwealth divestiture powers to break up companies that abuse their market power – i.e. abuse in the way the supermarket duopoly has ripped off both farmers and customers.

FUEL SECURITY

In another battle for transparency, Rex Patrick has discovered the truth about Australia's most vulnerable point – what if liquid fuels stopped coming from overseas. This is a quote from an article by Rex via Michael West Media entitled 'Empty tanks and bare shelves. Australia's fuel and supply security exposed.' Rex Patrick writes:

Australia's supply security in the event of a crisis goes way beyond toilet paper hoarding. And the Government doesn't want us to know about it. ... In 2013, retired Air Vice Marshal John Blackburn produced a report into Australia's Liquid Fuel Security for the NRMA. The report spelt out what would happen if Australian freight operations and logistics were shut down due to a lack of fuel. Food would quickly run out. We have just over a week of dry goods consumption available at our supermarkets and about a week for chilled and frozen foods. Pharmacies will start running out of medicine in about a week. And that's if there isn't panic buying, which COVID shows us would be highly likely. The thought of not having food in cupboards and fridges or prescription medicines would likely exercise people's minds a lot more than not having toilet paper. For hospitals, it's even worse. Hospitals typically hold a three-day reserve. Local petrol stations would run out of fuel in three days. Putting food and medicine aside, this would cripple the country economically. Our 'just in time' economy and society is absolutely dependent on uninterrupted fuel supplies.

Plus, we only have 26 days of in-country supply of diesel. In my view a crime equally bad as governments withholding this information since 2013 is that what they might have done, or didn't do, about this problem is still yet to be revealed. Consider this: if the US gets us involved in their planned hot war against China, then anything could stop our fuel supplies coming from overseas. If that happened we'd be toast before that month ended. The only solution to this vulnerability is to have our national fleet of vehicles be 100% electric; powered by local renewable energy.

> https://michaelwest.com.au/empty-tanks-and-bare-shelves-australias-fuel-and-supply-security-exposed/

DISASTER RESISTANT REGENERATIVE AGRICULTURE AND AQUAPONICS

We need disaster resistant agriculture, and Regenerative-organic agriculture, not the fertilizer and pesticide-dependent system we now have. And because we've covered so much arable land with suburbs (and are still alienating vast tracts of farm land with black-roofed houses creating more heat), we're going to need a lot of urban agriculture and greening of the cities. Everything that's not green-growing plants must be made white to restore Albedo.

We should bring fish-farming on-shore so the fish-excreta stops being pollution and becomes fertilizer for food crops. We must also stop robbing the marine ecosystem to provide fish food and instead grow crops for fish-food so we can sustainably grow fish that are good to eat. Omnivorous humans still need a source of high quality protein. Aquaponics must surely be less polluting than feed-lot fish, or feed-lot beef.

If these measures sound like too much regulation, bordering on state-control, they are not meant to be. The aim is to strike a balance between a responsible government that is responsive to society's needs while yet always heeding the voices of the people democratically – and not just at election time. The currency-issuing government may have a money tree in terms of treasury's almost limitless cheque account, but whatever services or works which our public money provides *do* require the use of real resources. Of course it's far better that public resources go to good things (e.g. health, education), not to bad things like war-making. This is where the people must have the power to regulate their government while their government exercises its powers to regulate fairness for the good of all the people. While *not* straying anywhere near Leninist statism, most Australians are heartily sick of the neoliberal privatisation and deregulation that allows the many to be shafted by the few.

ENERGY

Many of us take our use of energy for granted. We use heat energy to drive our old internal combustion vehicles and electrical energy for everything else. Up until now, most of that energy has come from the carbon-hydrogen bonds stored in ancient deposits, but that has to come to a rapid end. As stated earlier, rapid **electrification** from renewable sources is the best course open to us if we want to slow global heating as soon as possible. Saul Griffith, founder of Rewiring Australia, says we should electrify everything in our homes, workplaces and in our industries. Here's the link to the website:

> https://www.rewiringaustralia.org/

Obviously, electrifying our transport, trucks, buses, tractors etc with renewable energy is an urgent priority, but recent storms have shown how vulnerable our traditional grid system is. Poles and wires have been blown over or crushed by falling trees. Transmission lines are not only vulnerable to disasters, but they can start fires disastrously. With that top-of-mind, we need to be investing in disaster-resistant off-grid systems, especially for farms and rural communities where they can collect their own renewable energy and use it on-site. Micro and small grids in villages and towns will be more resilient than the macro state and national grids we're used to. Electrification of everything will need safe, efficient and affordable batteries. Fortunately there are a lot of clever people working to give us better batteries.

IMMIGRATION AND POPULATION

Immigration remains a good thing because diversity is a strength in any population, not a weakness (contrary to Trump). But we do need benign global population reduction while maximizing our carrying capacity without harming the biosphere further (e.g. by stopping deforestation and striving to restore ecosystem health). Ecologically, the world is overpopulated, so *population management* is vital. Rich countries must let our populations decline because we are such over-consumers, but poor countries must cure poverty so that more children are not needed for traditional aged care. Contraception should be a universal human right so that women can create only those children they need. If we give ourselves a right to life, then all children should also have the rights to be well and wanted. Matching our population to the true carrying capacity needs to be planned. Actions such as encouraging community gardens, supporting local, organic, permaculture and regenerative farming, plus educating people about food-growing and restoring Nature, can all help us be less dependent on the supermarket/fossil-fuel system and develop permanently-sustainable living. This will become ever more vital in the near future as 'hothouse Earth'/climate disasters and wars take their toll on globalization. Our present systems cannot continue, so we need to get serious about building safer homes and devising local food-growing systems that are resistant to disasters – and resilient in recovery.

SELF-SUFFICIENCY AND RECYCLING

Self-sufficiency and recycling of everything must be our aims. Our economy is now shockingly wasteful and unsustainable. We also need to electrify all our essential vehicles as a priority – ambulances, tractors, trucks, fire-fighting gear, etc – so we're not so dependent on imported liquid fuels. Electrifying and building resilience in our agriculture must be our top priorities, even higher than switching to disaster-proof homes, which is also vital. Renewables are our only hope for continued civilization, but they too come with an environmental cost, so we need to use less energy overall, power-down and shrink our impact on the biosphere to as little as possible. It's not going to be quick or easy to switch to a sustainable economy, but the sooner we get serious about it the sooner we will achieve it.

FALSE FEARS OF RECESSION AND CONTRACTION

The chief scare-tactic that governments and orthodox economists use to justify growthism is fear of the bogey-man 'recession'. Recession is defined as two consecutive quarters of negative GDP growth' (note: they can't even say 'six months of contraction'). The underlying fear is of the unemployment and subsequent poverty that is visited upon workers and their families in a recession – or in its prolonged version, a depression. Crises always hit the poor first and hardest. But a cynic would say that what the politicians really fear about the cessation of perpetual growth is the political back-lash from people who have been led to expect continual growth in their personal wealth – oh, and isn't it a shame about all those poor unemployed folks. As with everything, how badly a public policy (e.g. deliberate poverty), a climate disaster, galloping price rises, deliberate unemployment (the NAIRU myth), or an economic down-turn affects each person depends on the socio-economic position they are starting at. Recessions and depressions are as unequal in their affects as the social inequity they occur in. A recession rarely affects politicians or rich people directly, but politicians get criticised and profiteering has to slow, so nobody has relished the prospect of a dip in the business cycle, *aka* contraction, in the past. Consequently everyone has jumped on the (impossible) idea of endless growth as a way to avoid the feared pains of 'degrowth'. And most world governments have fallen into the political trap of '**justification by GDP**'. That's to say, justifying their continued power by showing robust economic growth.

An additional fear is that slowing production, with employers sacking workers, means less spending and less need for production so that a recession becomes a self-stoking disaster like the Great Depression of the 1930s. At that time, millions of people were thrust into unemployment and poverty. A big factor was not that there was a shortage of money or demand, but that there was a shortage of enough money *circulating* to keep people employed and sustained. In essence, it was hypovolaemic shock due to rich people, banks and governments not keeping the money moving and doing its job of paying for works and goods. Eventually, the policy prescriptions of Keynes and others were implemented in Roosevelt's New Deal. People realised that there was always plenty of work to be done if they looked for it, but it was up to the government to spend and tax so that people got employed and fed while the money started to circulate again to do its job. (Money also fails its job if it is merely kept in the accounts of rich people.) Friedman was right to say the Depression was worsened by constriction to the circulation of money, but wrong to say that money controls the economy when the reverse is more true. Quite evidently, economic activity determines the supply and velocity of money. New Deal jobs made the cash circulate. So, fears of contraction are **not** justified so long as the economic activity and funds are going fairly to where they are needed. Contraction can be fair, kind, and even rapid, provided resources are ***deliberately allocated*** to where they are needed.

Contraction (*aka* de-growth) and generous funding of essential public services do not need to be 'utterly at variance' with each other as neoliberal economists claim. *Appropriate* government spending is not inflationary and does not need to stop healthy economic contraction, even when funding on essentials is growing. All that is required is leadership and appropriate re-allocation of resources and funds away from militarism/war and billionaire-excess, back to fundamental human needs such as health, schools, etcetera.

There's a lot of unnecessary public argument about how constrained 'the budget' is and where our governments are going to find the money for the services we expect. While MMT has proven that currency-issuing governments can always find the money, this focus on money (the representation of value) is actually a distraction. For example, to diagnose a medical condition we don't get too hung up counting blood cells but look at the whole organism. So too we should focus on where the actual value is created (the real economic metabolism) and consider carefully where we want that value to go. Each nation has a finite quantity of labour and material resources. It may be hard to measure, but it is finite. Where do we want to deploy those resources? Do we really want to put it into nuclear submarines, or do we want to put it into health care and climate action? I put it to you that military equipment – that is virtually useless in a country the size of Australia – is a waste of those resources. Thinking of the scale of Australia, this huge desert island with 27 million people (less than the population of Tokyo, Delhi or Shanghai) clinging to its edges, our military amounts to just toys for the boys – it's a joke. If we stand back to look at the macro view and think of our nation in terms of being like a human body, then we wouldn't want it to be growing any useless belly fat (the military) while vital organs like our liver (e.g. agriculture) were starved of nutrition.

AUSTRALIA'S ECONOMIC BASE, AND TARIFFS

Unfortunately Australia doesn't have a significant economic base anymore. When our population was small the wool we sold brought in wealth. When I was young the apples grown in the Huon and shipped to Britain gave Tasmania the nickname of 'the Apple Isle', but that unsustainable situation stopped with the advent of the European Economic Community. Now Tasmania imports more food than it produces. I'm old enough to remember when John McEwen was leader of the Country party in coalition with Bob Menzies and part of their industry policy was called 'McEwenism', a combination of high tariff protection for local industry and plenty of government intervention in the economy. Tariffs are fine if your policy is isolationism, but if you want to trade in global markets then tariff barriers are a like shooting yourself in the foot. Trump doesn't get that yet. Free trade brings cheap goods, but pollutes the planet via shipping. Each nation should trade on its strengths. For example, the world needs cheap, quality, best-value electric vehicles and that's Chinese EVs, so North America and Europe putting tariffs on them to protect their own EV industries is counter-productive. On the other hand, a food-miles tax is only sensible to minimise absurdities like tinned tomatoes being shipped from Italy to Australia to be sold at half the price that local tomatoes are sold for.

What Australia does sell is the finite and depleting resources of stuff-that-gets-dug-up – Quarry Australia. Most of the profits for those mineral resources go overseas. US and UK investors are the biggest recipients. Since there is little taxation of the big transnational resource companies Australia isn't even putting aside a Sovereign Wealth Fund as Norway did with North Sea oil. At present our GDP growth is propped up by relatively high immigration of rich and well-educated folks from elsewhere (not refugees and/or asylum seekers, of course – they get sent to off-shore jails or kept in limbo for decades in order to have them discourage their poor and desperate relatives from trying to come to Australia too). At our peril Australia has shifted from being a producing economy to being a service economy. There are too many of us who are not producing anything of significant value. While inflating our population increases demand and pushes up national GDP for a while, the per-capita wealth and per-capita quality of life both fall with increased numbers of people. When the nation's carrying capacity is overrun, and with not enough productive self-sufficiency, then we are likely to see a recession or depression of monumental proportions. That's when a wise government and what I call a Household Care Cabinet will be needed.

ANOTHER WAY TO THINK OF ECONOMICS

The word 'economy' has its roots in the task of household care. Now, with all the challenges facing humanity, we need very good care for our community and for the world. Consequently economics needs to be about the 'household care' of communities, small and great. We need an economic system for need instead of greed. Right-wing folks hate all forms of redistribution, but since free-market capitalism only allocates resources to where they are 'greeded', it is overdue that we dump that system of economics – it is not a system for the proper care of any community (or global) 'household'. We need to see economics as working for the needs and care of everyone in our household/community.

ECONOMIC GROWTH = EXISTENTIAL THREAT

At the beginning, I said that economic growth is one of a handful of existential threats to almost every other living thing on this planet. This is because growth is accelerating global heating. If the dominoes of climate tipping-points keep falling at the rate they are, then the biosphere could go into rapidly rising, run-away heating, beyond 3 to 6 degrees, to 10, 20 degrees or more, then every living thing would die. Militarism and nuclear war could merely end our civilisation, but global heating is an existential threat to every species. Because growth is accelerating the heating, it is an absolute enemy to our continued existence; the one that makes every other 'threat' trivial.

Economic growth is defined as the accelerating increase (percentage rise = exponential rise) in the value and volume of our annual production. Politicians and economists love to talk about growth in the nation's Gross Domestic Product (GDP) and act like the economy is dying if there isn't growth. But even the main developer of the modern measure of GDP, Simon Kuznets, did not think it was a good measure of social or individual well-being – yet its fanatical admirers have turned it into the *only* significant indicator of our well-being. We must simply **_dump GDP_** as the measure of all things in the econo-political sphere.

Our language around economic growth is crazy. If it's not growing, the pundits say the economy is dead, or flat-lining, yet the economy is actually going very well, it's just not getting bigger and producing ever greater qualities of pollution and junk. Treasurer Chalmers and economists call the economy 'weak' or 'soft and subdued' if it's not growing enough (i.e. if people aren't making enough profit). They talk of negative growth rather than contraction. This obsession with GDP growth is a recent craze. People forget that civilization existed before growthist economics, before computers and the Internet – even before telephones! Folks just *assume* GDP has to grow. The fear of recession, depression, or degrowth is that there will be lots of people unemployed, but if the government handles it well then no one needs to suffer deprivation from degrowth. The government just has to keep real wealth going from where it's produced (in Nature) to where and to whom needs it.

If the economy is not growing people still get a return on their investment if they invest in something productive. It's just that they are not having their numbers increase so rapidly. The old economy where everyone is investing in someone else's Ponzi scheme cannot continue. Every nation must turn all its resources towards stopping global heating. And making a super-profit and making GDP grow have got to be things of the past.

Obviously, if the quantum of our production keeps growing (exponentially) each year, then 'growth' is also accelerating the increase in the volume of all forms of our pollution – thereby reducing every measure of our well-being, and every chance of our long-term survival. Growthism is mindless suicide! Whether it is CO_2, CH_4, plastics, toxins like PFAS, pesticides, herbicides, accumulating heat, or any of the other junk we are making and trashing, it is all driving the biosphere, and our agriculture, ever faster toward collapse.

AGRICULTURE

Agriculture is our Achilles' heel. When climate conditions cause major disruption to our food supplies, then our whole society is endangered. I grew up on a small farm where we knew there was an upper limit to the carrying capacity – the productivity – of a given quantity of adequate soil. It seems that politicians and economists ignore Nature's carrying capacity when they insist on ever more productivity and talk in funereal tones if the economy isn't growing. In fact the economy is fine, but if some people suffer more than others during a contraction it's because the losses are not fairly shared. As any farmer would know, if there is a shortage of stock-feed then the lack needs to be shared by the many, not just a few. A well run farm and the human body are both fair and egalitarian in nature.

Also as any farmer would know, the role of competition in modern economics is overrated. A healthy operating system depends on a great amount of co-operation. As well as the ACCC we need a co-operation authority. A motto for an egalitarian democracy might be the Buddhist aphorism: "Give up winning and losing, and find joy."

Growing up in the sixties (under Keynesian economics) Australia was far from being a fair egalitarian democracy, but it wasn't as radically unequal as it has become. Governments were in the job of public service before neoliberalism, and most people enjoyed the fact that the federal government owned the Commonwealth Bank, Qantas, and Telecom. A lot of service sectors are natural monopolies; like water supplies, food supplies, electricity supplies, health, pharmaceuticals, communications, transport, aviation, shipping, and banking. Public (i.e. state) ownership in these sectors is far from being state owned communism. Rather, government engagement with state business enterprises acts strongly to rein-in private profiteering. In all those fields there is room for private, worker-owned businesses. These give people commitment to the business of their livelihood and tend to hold public services to a standard. As E. F. Schumacher saw, worthwhile jobs are very important for enabling the happiness of people and for maintaining happy communities. I grew up in a worker owned business, the family farm, and we kids were the workers. Most farms were family businesses then. They may not have been as democratic as a modern co-op, but they were quite efficient. The corner stores were family owned and banking mutual co-ops could compete with the state owned bank. A mixed economy with many smaller business units is more feasible now since locally-collected renewable electricity is both possible and desirable. The obligation to have all private enterprises as worker owned democratic co-operatives (instead of capitalist, corporation, or sharebludger owned) will make society fairer, happier and more resilient to the effects of global heating. Ironically, Tasmania has a Department of State Growth when what we really need is a 'department of fair state contraction, global heating preparedness and survival', not a department dedicated to ever more economic growth and ecological destruction.

Growthism has the bizarre result that some economists call for increasing the world's population at this time when the whole world is overburdened with too many people. As Sir David Attenborough said, *I can't think of a single problem that wouldn't be easier to solve if there were fewer people.* This is the opposite of calling for population reduction from government coercion, but rather to restrain growthism in order to avoid mass deaths from wars and ecological breakdown.

Surely a minute's questioning of their own orthodoxy would show economists that growth of every sort is bad, not good. And yet on 8th March 2024, it was reported that China is still aiming for 5% growth each year, which would double everything in just 14 years. Such crazy economic growth targets might look good for a government that is still stuck in justification-by-growth, but it is ecologically reckless and probably impossible anyway.

Likewise, people speak of **green economic growth**, which is an ironic oxymoron. As far as the biosphere is concerned, we cannot have increasing industrial production, rising consumption and worsening pollution and imagine that's an improvement. But if by green growth you mean growing more food and trees and making the desserts bloom, then fine, but until then any talk of green economic growth is another form of climate denial.

Denialism of global heating and our current growth-economics are inextricably mixed. The Growthists want to keep business and their wallets growing as usual, but global heating means that's impossible. Some have talked of a '**Green Wall Street**' where privateers can chase profits in environmentally friendly pursuit of profit and thereby save the world. But this is also a contradiction in terms. The related idea of **Green Capitalism** is another oxymoron. The ethos of the profiteer may be irreconcilably opposed to the ethos of those who seek a fair, democratic and sustainable green-peace. The capitalist, imperialist, colonialist ethos is to exploit whatever they can, leave the pollution, take the profit and run away home. They privatise the profit and socialise the pollution. It's impossible for polluting profiteering to save the world from the pollution of profiteering. The cognitive dissonance caused by this dilemma makes denialism the only escape hatch, but it's only an escape from reality. Our hyper-industrial, exponentially growing, eco-destructive way of living is simply unsustainable and must stop. As US author Edward Abbey said, growth for the sake of growth is the ideology of cancer. Our linear, industrial, consumer-capitalism is a cancer in the body of Gaia. How is it that so many people have failed to see this obvious equation?

Of course, many people *have* seen the absurdity of growth-economics on our finite planet. Here in Tasmania we have Sustainable Living Tasmania and many other groups. More widely in Australia, there's a plethora of groups working for a sustainable way of living. There's Economic Reform Australia (ERA), Sustainable Population Australia (SPA), the Council for the Human Future, and numerous others. Internationally, examples include the Post-Growth Institute which describes itself as 'an international, not-for-profit organization working to enable collective wellbeing within ecological limits', and there's the Growth-Busters group led by Dave Gardner in the US who put it this way, *economics has met the enemy, and it is economics*. There are also numerous books on the subject, and just a few examples follow: *Small is Beautiful* E. F. Schumacher (1973), *The Limits to Growth* Meadows x 2, Randers, & Behrens (1975), *Growth Fetish* Clive Hamilton (2003), *The End of Growth* Richard Heinberg (2011), *Prosperity Without Growth* Tim Jackson (2017), *Less is More: How Degrowth Will Save the World* Jason Hickel (2020), *Enough is Enough* Dietz & O'Neill, and *The Future is Degrowth: A Guide to a World Beyond Capitalism* Schmelzer, Vetter & Vansintjan (2022). (Note the euphemism 'degrowth' instead of the more accurate term 'contraction'.)

SO MANY people have tried to tell the world that perpetual growth in a finite world is unsustainable, yet orthodox economists, business leaders, and politicians continue their insane faith in it. Several 20th century economists pointed to the impossibility of endless growth and resource depletion, including Ernst Schumacher, Nicholas Georgescu-Roegen, and Kenneth Boulding. Many since have pointed out this obvious fact, but still the dogma of economic growth continues. My book tries to examine reasons for the persistence of this absurdity, and many of our other maladaptive behaviours, but governments, state and federal, from China to the US and back, are unable to let go of growthism because they have huge 'sunk cost' in '***justification by growth***' – which is to say they justify themselves by constantly pointing to a rising GDP. (And Australian governments have detrimentally propped up their GDP – and suppressed wages – with very high net immigration.)

There are many other reasons for the inertia that resists all pro-adaptive change (including effective climate action), but growthism is buttressed by economists, journalists, and politicians speaking as if an economy is 'stalled', dead and buried if it isn't doubling in production fast enough. Witness the foolish laments of the IMF regarding 'only' 3% growth, this year, just as the IPCC is telling us we may have missed our last chance to save our species! Yet GDP growth is so clearly a *negative* measure of well-being, especially in our grossly unequal societies. Consequently, we urgently need politicians and economists who are brave enough to make the ideological and legislative U-turn that our survival depends upon.

We must 'power-down' and use much less and waste much less of everything. As many have said, the best energy is the energy you don't use. And the best mineral resource is the one you've recovered by recycling. Degrowth need not be frightening for our standard of living if we focus on a fair quality of life for all. There are those who want to make it a big bogey-man. At least one denialist American has made the ridiculous and ignorant assertion that 'Degrowth is Communism' – that shows ignorance of both degrowth and communism. His claim that 'capitalism is unsustainable, but socialism can't produce' is nonsense. Nature is the ultimate source of all production. The machinations of homo-faber (man the maker) all depend on Earth's resources. We DO need to reduce the stuff that we're producing and the pollution that we're causing, but degrowth is NOT Leninist/Stalinism, it is survivalism. We don't need sustainable growth capitalism – that's impossible – instead we need sustainable, Earth-responsive humanism.

The word that economists and politicians dare not speak, 'contraction', must become central to our economics. As mentioned much earlier, in *Liberation Economics* I use the human body as a rough analogy to our obese and ballooning economies that need to lose weight evenly. Fair national and global contraction can happen like a body loses weight: by restricting consumption and re-allocating resources. This requires governments of all levels to commit to fairness, to economic and environmental justice. It also needs all governments to commit to international justice in the form of rich countries lifting poor countries out of poverty, especially as it's the poorer countries that will struggle to recover from climate disasters the most. But as climate scientists have pointed out, the global nature of climate change means that we may all become climate refugees.

A global peace treaty to save the biosphere is vital, and redirecting all military resources toward Earth-saving is also vital. After all, war-making is by far the biggest waste of human and material resources globally. Violence begets violence and war-making makes war, but peace also creates peace.

Governments must take responsibility, intervene in rudderless, inequality-creating markets and not leave public-policy to the privateers. Earth-saving also means taxing the super-rich and corporations, and switching the economics of consumerism to 100% conservation. The task is to convert the fat (in the system) into muscle, to restrict extravagant and wasteful consumption, reduce high levels of polluting, and employ millions of people in recycling, cleaning up our act, and growing the vegetation to replace all that we've destroyed.

EMPLOYMENT

The big problem with winding down our industrialized economy is employing all those who currently depend on that industrial system. That's where we have to transition our economy most radically. We have to shift from a profit motivation to a survival motivation. As we battle the damage being done by worsening heat-related disasters, and work to reverse the heating as best we can, we will need a lot of people and resources employed in these tasks on behalf of our communities. And since there'll be no profit in those for the privateers, then it must be our governments that pay. The rest of us will need to be turning our efforts toward providing food and shelter for our families independent of the old supply chains. We won't be able to afford socialism for the military any longer because events will force us into socialism for survival.

POPULATION

Regrettably, despite electrifying everything as fast as we can, with renewable energy, and despite reducing our emissions as fast as we can (if we do), and as painful as it will be to some, we also have to reduce our global populations as fast as is benignly possible. Right-wing pundits treat this as a horrifying notion, but why? Is it because a non-coercive lowering of our fertility rates is beyond their imagination, or is it that fewer 'consumers' will reduce their rabid profiteering and end their ecocidal drive to grow ever richer?

Our global population is still growing exponentially at about 0.9% annually. Between 2022 and 2023 it grew by approximately 70 million, and the year since then has added another 74 million people. We are destroying life on this planet at an ever increasing rate. There has been a 73% drop in wildlife populations in only the 50 years between 1970 and 2020. Five million fish are killed every minute by the global fishing industry. Our ever greater numbers are causing an ever greater decline in Nature's ability to feed us. The carrying capacity of Spaceship Earth has simply been exceeded by far too many of us being alive at this time. And sad to say, we either reduce our numbers the easy way, by limiting the number of children we conceive, or else Nature will reduce our numbers the hard way – by washing us away, destroying our crops and livestock, starving us, burning our homes, and being the trigger for all the climate survivors to be in conflict with all the climate refugees.

Yes, you will hear the growthists argue that global heating is not real, or even if it is then it won't have much effect, as the Nobel Prize-winning American economists Thomas Schelling and William Nordhaus apparently claimed in a 1983 report entitled 'Changing Climate, Report of the Carbon-Dioxide Assessment Committee'. On rising CO_2 Schelling is said to have written:

> *Today, little of our gross domestic product* [GDP] *is produced outdoors, and therefore, little is susceptible to climate. Agriculture and forestry are less than 3 percent of total output, and little else is much affected. Even if agricultural productivity declined by a third over the next half-century, the per capita GNP we might have achieved by 2050 we would still achieve in 2051. Considering that agricultural productivity in most parts of the world continues to improve ... it is not at all certain that the net impact on agriculture will be negative or much noticed in the developed world.*

What Schelling did not acknowledge is that the climate-exposed 3% of their GDP measure supports the entire other 97% of human activity. Without a healthy agricultural sector nothing else is possible. First the prices for scarce food goes right up where only the rich can buy it, then the whole economy collapses when everyone is starving. Schelling doubted that the net affects on agriculture would even be 'much noticed' in the developed world – what about the less developed world? Plus, if large chunks of the world's agriculture is blown and/or washed away, how will we live? This nonsense became popular with politicians because it meant they didn't have to rein-in the use of fossil fuels and they could continue unthinkingly with their 'justification-by-growth' econo-politics. Econo-babble triumphed over science.

Economic growth (often fuelled by high immigration or schemes for higher birth rates) has been used by governments to claim economic success and to justify themselves, but this must no longer be the case because growth is genuinely killing us. You'll hear growthists claim that it's been growth capitalism that has lifted billions out of poverty. But while it's true that many are no longer in poverty, globally, it is not Neoliberal capitalism but the ever-burgeoning deployment of burnable fossils whose energy has built our industrial civilization. It's ironic that it is the pollution and destruction wrought by that same life-improving deployment that is killing the biosphere and may bring all our lives to their end. So if you hear any politician or economist laud the virtues of population growth or economic growth, you can be sure they are either mad, thoughtlessly stupid, or both!

But as mentioned above, even as that IPCC report was published, the International Monetary Fund was lamenting that the world's annual economic growth was going to be 'only' 3% – and this bemoaning at a time when we should be contracting most frantically, not doubling our pollution and everything every 23.45 years (the doubling-time at 3% pa)! What do they think they are doing? Surely the IMF sees how 'exponential-growth-economics' and 'the Great Acceleration' are just accelerating humanity toward our sui-generis extinction? Has the Secretary General of the United Nations not spoken clearly enough? And even if global heating, grinding poverty, and rising extreme-inequality were *not* problems for Australia and every other country, the absurdity of this 'growth fetish' or 'growthism' alone should compel a radical re-invention of our whole system of economics. I wonder repeatedly, what severity and frequency of weather extremes will it take before the doubters and science-class drop-outs agree that radical action is needed?

On the 1st of August 2024, the world marked Overshoot Day. Every year it is coming earlier. It's the day on which it is estimated humanity has used all of Nature's productivity and where it is said that we begin to draw down on the so-called Natural capital of the world. But Nature's capital is not like cash in the bank capital. Ecology doesn't work like that. If you take more than an ecological system can give then the productivity of the system degrades so that less can be taken in future. Overshoot day signifies by how much we are exceeding the carrying-capacity of Earth's biosphere. This global overshoot is caused by our accelerating over-consumption and over-population. As stated above, these are being enabled by our unrestrained use of fossil fuels under the demands of greed and growth capitalism. We have been exceeding the carrying-capacity of Spaceship Earth for so many years that now the life-support systems of our planet are starting to fail. The only way to save ourselves from here is to reverse all the damage that's happening as a result of growthism, and to institute a fair process of contraction and restoration. It's not that we have to stop work, lose jobs, or become poor as we power-down our over-production and trash-focused economies, but rather that we have to work a lot harder at different jobs, new jobs that help to securely provide ourselves with food, to build disaster-proof homes, to make our cultural activities less destructive, to make our societies kinder and more-tolerant, plus ensuring world peace, and restoring Nature.

There is reason for hope, and *hope we must*, because the fossil fuel corporations are now weaponising our despair and doubt in order to again fight climate action and adaptation. Here's a video that goes through some of the issues:

> We WILL Fix Climate Change! (youtube.com)

As George Monbiot pointed out, the two biggest things we can do is leave fossil fuels in the ground and stop farming animals, but there's much more we **can** do. It won't be easy and contraction will surely lead to lower 'standards' of living for some in the rich world. However, the restoration of Nature will lead to higher 'quality of life' for billions of us. We need to vote at the ballot box for people who believe the science and also vote with our wallets to buy sustainable goods and not buy the planet-wrecking products and services. As this video concludes, if we do solve global heating everyone will be a bit unhappy, but that will be okay. Better that almost all of us change our ways than for all of us to be dead. Please watch this video on the problem, and consider the economics:

> Can YOU Fix Climate Change? (youtube.com)

The alternative to this semi-benign adaptation will be very malign decades during which this burning spaceship destroys all its human passengers.

CONCLUSIONS

Economic growth is wrong. Inequality is wrong. Endless price increases (inflation) are wrong. Involuntary unemployment is wrong. The high cost of borrowed money is wrong. Monetarism is wrong. Neoliberal economics is wrong. Rent-seeking corporations are pirates. Privatization and outsourcing are wrong. Small government ideology is wrong. Landlordism is unfair, so renting should be phased out. Worker ownership cooperatives must replace corporations and 'bosses'. Private, high-profit, low-service banks – or any privatized public service or natural monopoly (e.g. health, education) – should be nationalised. Slave-wages and conditions should never exist. Power hierarchies must be minimized. Making war is insane and inhumanly evil. Socialism for the Military-Industrial-Fossil-Fuel Complex is wrong. Floating currencies and international purchasing-power disparities are cruelly unfair. Extracting and dissipating every last natural resource is just stupid greed. Using nuclear power now but leaving the clean-up to our descendants is an intergenerational crime. Degrading and polluting Nature is destroying our life-support systems and amounts to global suicide. It doesn't have to be that way. These things are *not necessary* and can be easily fixed. All it will take is the political drive to do it.

We must put all our efforts and economic resources into these tasks: winding down production while also building the overdue transformation to all-electric; growing trees and greening everything; stopping all waste and pollution; ending poverty & inequality; stopping all needless military rivalry via #WorldPeaceNow and preparing for highly destructive climate change. If we put as much energy into these as we put into sports, and as many resources as we've been putting into military machines, war games and wars, then we could preserve the liveability of Spaceship Earth for our children and for all our descendants.

This is our heaven, there is no other. Deity-belief is fooling ourselves – we must become as rational and civilised as we can – that's to say our most sublime, empathic and caring selves, not our savage, murdering and destructive selves. If we get our minds and our actions going 100% towards survival we can change course to avert most of the worst outcomes.

There is not yet enough sense of urgency to energize these necessary changes, but the time will soon come when radical action will be demanded by the majority of people. Global demilitarisation may seem impossible now, but its time must come. The solutions to the cost of living, energy transition, and re-greening are there for any courageous national government. Here's a wish-list for Australia's federal government that I prepared earlier.

These are not in order of priority, but need to be enacted simultaneously.

1. Stop all subsidies and support for Fossil Fuel corporations, and switch urgently to the decentralized, cheapest, most efficient energy via 100% renewables-electric economy, only do it faster than we are now doing it.

2. Immediately raise welfare up to the poverty line (double Jobseeker again) and ensure all income supports and social services are properly funded.
3. Legislate prices and wages justification via a new authority to stop all price-gouging, profiteering, and insane top salaries.
4. Tax the corporations and the very-rich – not the poor.
5. Legislate divestiture and anti-merger laws in order to stop the rip-off of suppliers and customers by vertically-integrated corporations – and to break up the billionaire-owned media.
6. Abolish the current monetarist RBA and get Keynesian and MMT economists into a service-focused, re-nationalised Commonwealth Bank, or Post-Office bank, that serves people not profits. All other (private) banks to be 100% capitalised and/or make all non-government banks public-owned via cooperative, mutual, customer-ownership.
7. Restore Medicare so we can have free health care again, and add dental care to Medicare.
8. Make all education free too, and pay back HECS debts.
9. Steadily buy back all debt instruments, bonds etc (i.e. alternative IOUs) to stop the flow of public money to the rich and to the banks.
10. Fairly slow economic activity and ensure simultaneous contraction *and* full employment.
11. Deploy a national job guarantee – e.g. people restoring Nature, planting and nurturing trees.
12. Give the states and territories the money they need or else do their tasks like health and education properly and totally instead.
13. Discourage the use and extraction of all fossil fuels; impose fuel rationing if necessary.
14. Establish pollution reduction infrastructure to protect the oceans; phase out all single use plastics, pesticides and herbicides. Ban all native forest logging and land-clearing. Recycle everything.
15. Promote and fund regenerative organic agriculture, permaculture, polyculture and aquaponics, and support all food-producers.
16. Establish an Environment Protection Agency that puts a climate veto on *every* ecologically harmful 'development'. Ensure the EPA can prosecute offenders, and that a *Duty of Care for Future Generations* clause overrides everything all Australian governments do.
17. Cancel AUKUS and stop pouring public money into US & UK submarines etc. Cut all other military spending, and work to abolish all militarism. Use diplomacy to make world peace, then

reinvest the Peace Dividend in global heating resilience and reversal, plus retrain and redeploy the military personnel into disaster rescue and recovery.
18. Develop import-substitution systems and supply-chain shortening measures.
19. Restore public services by re-nationalisation essential services such as electricity, water, communications, health, aged & child care (for example, train and employ as many public servants as needed to make service-providers such as Centrelink functional, kind, and not robot/computer-dominated any longer.
20. Maximise integrity and ensure fully-open, accountable, uncorrupt government.
21. Reduce all advertising to essentials-only in order to minimise unnecessary consumption (the way for a body to lose weight is to reduce consumption; likewise an economy). Abolish all gambling, as far as possible.
22. De-market housing, make a safe home a human right, build millions of public-owned homes and establish hire-purchase for homes.
23. Peg the value of the Australian currency to an hour of labour in order to help stop inflation and work towards establishing international Purchasing Power Parity.
24. Legislate for transition to compulsory worker ownership of all private enterprise.

(These last two will make money markets and share markets obsolete; plus the labour market will also vanish as a job guarantee and good vocational training are implemented.)

PREPARING

Around the world, people are preparing for the collapse of civilization; they're called Preppers. Preparing for ecological collapse alone or as a family is difficult, but it's better to be preppers as a community, better still to react as a nation, if possible, and best of all to work to slow global heating and to stop war-mongering as a world community. However, responding to existential threats as a world community requires world peace now, or as soon as possible. War-making militarism and growth economics may seem impossible to stop, but these evils are made by men and can be unmade by men. They could easily be stopped as our first actions in our urgent damage-control mission for Earth. We can just stop doing them and work harder at doing the fair, caring, co-operative and sustainable things instead.

With our 'growthist' economy going exactly the wrong way, and global heating about to wreck the world's ability to produce food, every government has plenty of reasons to proclaim ***an indefinite national emergency*** and to enact emergency powers in order to right these wrongs and pull our societies down into truly kind and sustainable shape.

The rapid changes of the past 70 years are called 'the great acceleration'. But the changes, the growth, and especially the pollution they've caused, have driven us to the brink of our own extinction. So the great un-equalizing acceleration must now become the radically equalizing deceleration. We need an entirely new economic and cultural paradigm to make it happen. That demands a mind-set that is co-operative, caring, peace-loving, nurturing, and conserving; not our competitive, exploitive, extractive, ecocidal, militaristic, and destructive behaviour as we've been doing up till now. The economics of fairness, contraction, and restoration requires peace, not war, ecological action, not money-focused entertainments, reason not faith, truth not lies, collective compassion not tribal fascism, mutual respect not bigotry, peace-making not power-playing or enmity, fairness not injustice. It's right now that our whole species needs that radically equalizing deceleration – survival not suicide.

Thank you

POST SCRIPT

I'm dismayed to see our roads hosting a rash of super-sized, 4WD petrol-guzzlers – that the ALP government has made exempt from emissions regulations – because it means there are many men (with adequacy issues) who not only deny climate science but are also keen to spend big money in defiance of our urgent need to transition out of fossil fuels.

Further to that, the world's military-industrial complex will hate moves for world peace and international co-operation; Americans will hate opposition to their fanatical militarism and delusional exceptionalism; the commercial banks will hate their thieving profiteering being called out; the RBA will hate having its job of feeding public money to private banks and rich people curtailed; the Murdoch media will hate being sued for their climate-science denial and our fully justified moves to throw them out of Australia; the fossil fuel corporations already hate moves to wind them down; the rich will hate being taxed fairly; the business-as-usual lobby will hate fair price controls and worker ownership; the Liberal/Labor duopoly and its bureaucracy will hate criticism of their neoliberal fascism; the drivers of the super-sized utes will hate fuel rationing; the religionists will hate being asked to be rational; all of us who are addicted to high technology and totally dependent on the supermarket system will hate having to be more low-tech practical, and to be more self sufficient and sustainable in our ways of living. The aggregate of resistance to change is enormous and dangerous! For these reasons the necessary transition won't happen until people are forced to change by external circumstances such as wars and natural disasters. Being realistic, no government will be able to persuade everyone to adapt before there's no other alternative. One wonders what magnitude of disaster it will take for the majority of people to change to sustainable, peaceful, and non-polluting livelihoods on Spaceship Earth.

For the first time in Earth's approximately four and a half billion year history, just one species has become so dominant and destructive as to cause a mass extinction (the 6th) and what this species has set in motion may yet make this planet uninhabitable for *any* life.

That's down to us. But if we're **not** going to prepare and adapt as a globe or even as a community, then our one remaining task is to ensure at least the near-term survival of our loved ones while still striving against probability to keep civil society going and save as many other people and other living beings as possible. This is our dual role: public pressure for change and private preparation for the almost certain collapse of civilization.

Copyright © Bob Elliston 2024
bob_elliston@yahoo.com.au

Published by Chapter Seven
ABN 32 871 066 846

Paperback ISBN: 978-1-7638189-0-3
eBook ISBN: 978-1-7638189-1-0

All rights reserved.
This book is copyright apart from any fair dealing for the purpose of private study research, criticism, or review as permitted under the Copyright Act.
No part may be reproduced by any process without permission of the author.

Printer: IngramSpark

www.ingramcontent.com/pod-product-compliance
Lightning Source LLC
Chambersburg PA
CBHW052144070526
44585CB00017B/1960